William Odling

Lectures on Animal Chemistry

Delivered at the Royal College of Physicians

William Odling

Lectures on Animal Chemistry
Delivered at the Royal College of Physicians

ISBN/EAN: 9783337069872

Printed in Europe, USA, Canada, Australia, Japan

Cover: Foto ©ninafisch / pixelio.de

More available books at **www.hansebooks.com**

LECTURES
ON
ANIMAL CHEMISTRY

DELIVERED AT

THE ROYAL COLLEGE OF PHYSICIANS.

BY

WILLIAM ODLING, M.B., F.R.S.

FELLOW OF THE COLLEGE;
LECTURER ON CHEMISTRY AT SAINT BARTHOLOMEW'S HOSPITAL.

LONDON:
LONGMANS, GREEN, AND CO.
1866.

TO

THOMAS WATSON, M.D., F.R.S.

PRESIDENT OF THE ROYAL COLLEGE OF PHYSICIANS

THESE LECTURES

HONOURED AT THE TIME OF THEIR DELIVERY

BY HIS

FRIENDLY EXPRESSIONS OF INTEREST AND APPROVAL

ARE NOW

WITH HIS KIND PERMISSION

RESPECTFULLY AND GRATEFULLY DEDICATED

BY

HIS OBLIGED SERVANT

THE AUTHOR

manuscript, and further revising the published reports of the 'Chemical News,' I have made it my constant object to give such an account of modern Organic Chemistry as should, with a moderate amount of attention, be profitable and even interesting to those who are not chemists. In other words, I have striven throughout, whether or not successfully, to render my subject popular in the legitimate sense, by making it generally intelligible.

I need scarcely say that these lectures are not meant to exert any direct influence upon points of medical practice. I hope, however, they may assist in convincing the profession at large of the necessity for regarding vital phenomena from a chemical point of view; and in promoting among students, especially those about to graduate, the knowledge of a highly important though much neglected branch of natural science.

St. Bartholomew's Hospital:
March 1, 1866.

CONTENTS.

LECTURE I.

PROVINCE OF CHEMISTRY. TYPES OF CONSTITUTION AND RELATIONSHIP. AMIDATED ORGANIC COMPOUNDS. 1

LECTURE II.

DOCTRINE OF RESIDUES. APLONE AND POLYMERONE BODIES. ORGANIC GROUPS AND SERIES. 21

LECTURE III.

DESTRUCTION AND CONSTRUCTION OF COMPLEX MOLECULES. NATURE OF NITROGENOUS COMPOUNDS. OXIDES OF HYDROGEN AND CARBON. . 46

LECTURE IV.

FORCES CONCERNED IN VITAL ACTIONS. ACTUAL AND POTENTIAL ENERGY. ARTIFICIAL SYNTHESIS OF ORGANIC BODIES. 66

LECTURE V.

DYNAMIC VALUE OF MUSCLE OXIDATION. INTERMEDIATE PRODUCTS OF TISSUE-METAMORPHOSIS. 97

LECTURE VI.

URIC ACID AND ITS CONGENERS. CHEMICAL ACTION OF ALTERATIVE MEDICINES. 126

Errata.

Page 83, line 5 from foot, *for* $C_3H_4O_2$ (Acetic) *read* $C_2H_4O_2$ (Acetic).

Page 92, line 19 from top, *for* $(C_2H_5)H.CNS$ *read* $(C_2H_5)CNS$.

ANIMAL CHEMISTRY.

LECTURE I.

Introductory remarks on recently established general principles in chemistry—Statical chemistry concerned only with the composition of parts; with the different kinds of matter of which all the tissues and fluids of the body are composed—Dynamical chemistry concerned with the changes of composition undergone by various parts from time to time—Physical changes, as of a piece of iron, contrasted with its chemical changes—Special reference of chemistry to past and future states of bodies—Every action of living body attended by changes of chemical composition—Recent advances in chemistry of tissue-products—Leucine a result of the natural metamorphosis of glandular tissue—Its artificial formation, destructively and constructively—Taurine a constituent of bile, &c.—Its artificial production from carbon, hydrogen, nitrogen, oxygen, and sulphur—Chemical types of construction and double decomposition—Compounds of hydrogen with other three gaseous elements—Establishment of molecular formulæ for hydrochloric acid HCl, water H_2O, and ammonia H_3N—Existence in two volumes of gaseous hydrochloric acid, water, and ammonia, of one, two, and three volumes of hydrogen respectively, in addition to one volume of chlorine, or oxygen, or nitrogen—Monhydrides, dihydrides, and trihydrides in general, and their derived chlorides—Existence of analogous mono-, di-, and tri-chlorides of metals deduced from specific heats of respective metals, &c.—Mutual relations of chlorides, hydrates, and amides, both of elements and groupings—Interchangeability of comparable residues (Cl from HCl, HO from $H.HO$, and H_2N from $H.H_2N$) in great variety of compounds—Chlorinated, hydrated, and ammoniated forms of the same primitive bodies—Many complex nitrogenous tissue-products only the ammoniated forms of comparatively simple bodies—Urea, glycocine, and taurine the ammoniated forms of the carbonic, acetic or glycolic, and isethionic acids respectively—Mixed hydrate-amides.

(1.) Mr. President and Gentlemen,—It has been, I am well aware, the traditional policy of this College, in its character of a learned body, to foster the cultivation of natural science for its own sake, irrespective of any immediate advantage accruing to medical practice, and regardless even of the ultimate advantage which, sooner or later, must accrue from every addition to our knowledge of the phenomena of life. I therefore make no apology, Sir, for directing your attention to topics of which the present interest, at any rate, is more scientific than practical, relying upon the favour ever extended to pure science within these walls—relying still more confidently upon the prospective ability of science to repay your favour many fold.

I feel, however, that I ought to apologise for venturing to discuss in this presence some of the more rudimentary principles of chemical philosophy; but the circumstance that these principles, despite their rudimentary character, are yet of very recent introduction must furnish my excuse. Indeed, it is only within the last fifteen years or so that chemical facts have been in any large measure subordinated to chemical principles, and only within a very few years past that these principles have been consistently developed and generally acknowledged. But the result of this development and recognition is already apparent: for we find that, notwithstanding the continuous accumulation of recorded experiment, and the continuous discovery of new and complex bodies with a rapidity at which even the most impassive are amazed, chemistry is daily becoming less and less a science of detail, more and more a science of generality, to such an extent indeed, that, in my opinion, a student beginning the study of chemistry now, with a view to make himself acquainted with the knowledge of his own day, has a far less difficult task before him than had his predecessor of twenty years ago, despite the then limited range of chemical inquiry. To some extent, therefore, I am forced, especially in this introductory lecture, to devote a considerable proportion of my allotted time to an enunciation of certain general truths of more or less recent establishment. But, in order that we may set out from the same standpoint, I must beg still further to trespass upon your attention by reminding you briefly of the special province of chemical science, and the special character of chemical phenomena.

(2.) If we examine any ordinary plant or animal, we find in it a great number of parts or organs—root and stem, and bark and leaves, and flowers and fruit, or bones and ligaments, and muscles and viscera, and nerves and vessels. If we examine any one of these parts more minutely, we find that it also is made up of parts differing from one another, and so disposed towards one another as to present evidence of arrangement or organisation. Proceeding a little further, we find that each of these parts has a definite composition, and that the composition of the different parts is, to some extent, at any rate, independent both of their individual structure and mutual co-ordination. We find, for instance, very differently characterised tissues composed mainly of fibrin or albumen, others of gelatin or chondrin, others of fat, and others, again, of phosphate of lime. Now, chemistry does not concern itself at all with the structure and arrangement of parts, but treats only of their composition. It distinguishes between the different kinds of matter of which all bodies whatsoever are composed, whether living or dead, structural or structureless, mineral or organic. In particular, it teaches us as physicians the composition of every tissue and fluid of the human body, and of every external agent by which that body is affected—the air we breathe, the water we drink, the food by which we are nourished, the medicines by which we are healed, and the poisons by which we are destroyed.

(3.) But a knowledge of the composition of bodies is, after all, only the statical or secondary object of chemical inquiry; for, in common with physics, chemistry has primary reference to the varied existence of matter in time, and to the series of changes which it manifests. We have regard to a body not only as it now is, but as it has been, as it may hereafter be, the changes it has undergone in time past, the changes which it may undergo in time to come. Confining our attention to a single object—this piece of iron, for instance—let us consider how varied have been the states of its existence at different times. We know that it has been at rest and in motion; it has been silent and sonorous; it has been luminous and obscure, hot and cold, liquid and solid, magnetic and non-magnetic, electrical and non-electric. But throughout all these changes of rest and motion, sound and silence, heat and cold, &c., the individual piece of metal has continued one and the same; it has been composed throughout of identically the same matter. Now, so long as a body continues to be one and the same body—so long, in fact, as its composition remains unaltered—so long do all the changes which it manifests belong to the province of physics, and not to the province of chemistry. For this piece of iron to undergo a chemical change, it must cease to be a piece of iron, and become some other body —rust of iron, or vitriol of iron, or tincture of iron, or Prussian blue, or clot of blood, or some one of many hundred different combinations. Looking, then, to the chemistry of this piece of iron, we have regard to the state of ironstone in which it existed before it became metallic iron, and to the many different non-metallic states in which it may hereafter exist. The dynamical interest of a body has reference to its existence in time, to its past and future variations of state, even more than to its present condition. I venture to impress this point particularly on your attention, that while chemistry treats of the composition of bodies, it has special reference to their changes in composition. Now, when we consider that every action of the living body, every growth, every waste, every secretion, every movement, and even every thought is attended by, and consequent upon, a change of chemical composition, we perceive, in an instant, how much the future of physiology must depend on the progress of chemical research—how only the iatro-chemist, if I may so call him, can ever hope to understand the varied series of actions, healthy and morbid, which are continually taking place in the living organism. The chemistry, then, of any animal tissue—of a piece of muscle, for instance, no less than a piece of iron—has reference to its origin and metamorphoses. The chemist looks equally to its past and its future—to the pabulum from which it was formed, and to the products into which it is ever changing.

(4.) Of late years the chemistry of animal products has made very great advances. In the table before you are written up the names and somewhat complicated formulæ of a few of these compounds, most of which occur in the animal body, as results of the natural metamorphosis of its several tissues. Now, despite the complexity of many of these bodies, the intimate constitution of even the most complicated of them is fairly well understood, and in many cases so well understood that the bodies themselves can be actually built up by the chemist in his laboratory without having any recourse whatever to organic nature.

Animal Products

$C H_5 N$	Methylamine
$C H_4 N_2 O$	Urea
$C_2H_5 N O_2$	Glycocine
$C_2H_7 N S O_3$	Taurine
$C_3H_6 N_6$	Melamine
$C_3H_7 N_2O_2$	Sarcosine
$C_4H_9 N_3O_2$	Kreatine
$C_6H_{13}N O_2$	Leucine
$C_9H_{11}N O_3$	Tyrosine

Let me direct your attention to one or two of these more particularly. Here, for instance, is leucine, a white crystalline body, consisting of 6 atoms of carbon, 13 of hydrogen, 1 of nitrogen, and 2 of oxygen. Now, leucine is a product of the use, and consequent waste or metamorphosis, of glandular tissue. It is found in decoctions of glandular tissue, more particularly of the spleen and pancreas; and also occurs occasionally as an abnormal constituent of urine. It may be made artificially in the flask or crucible by the breaking up of muscle, ligament, skin, horn, hair, feathers, and a variety of other animal substances; but so well is the constitution of this complex tissue-product understood, that leucine can now be formed, not only destructively by the breaking up of more complex bodies, but constructively by a synthesis of less complex organic bodies quite independently of animal life. It may be produced, for example, by the combination with one another of water, valerianic aldehyd,* and prussic acid, as shown in the table; and in several other ways.

H_2O	Water
$C_5H_{10}O$	Valer-aldehyd
$C H N$	Prussic acid
$C_6H_{13}NO_2$	Leucine

(5.) The case of taurine, $C_2H_7NSO_3$, is even more striking. Like leucine, it has been found in glandular tissue, more particularly of the lung; but its chief source is the bile, where it exists conjugated with cholic acid, to form what is known as tauro-cholic acid; though whether the constituent taurine of this acid is really formed by the liver, or merely extracted by the liver from the blood of the portal vein, is not, I believe, satisfactorily ascertained. But the constitution of this highly complex organic body, containing, as you see, carbon, hydrogen, nitrogen, sulphur, and oxygen, is so exactly understood that it can easily be put together in the laboratory, and from such well-known bodies as sulphuric acid, alcohol, and ammonia, each of which again is capable of being produced from its constituent elements; so that we may actually form this most interesting organic product, taurine, out of sulphur, charcoal, oxygen, hydrogen, and nitrogen, by processes which I hope to bring under your notice more particularly in a subsequent lecture. I might make similar remarks with regard to the greater number of the other products included in the table. Instead, however, of entering at once upon the consideration of these and similar compounds, I propose to occupy the remainder of this lecture with an account of certain bodies of a much simpler character. I mean those fundamental combinations that serve as types to which the above class of bodies and the great majority of organic as well as mineral compounds are more or less directly referrible. The recognition of these types, with the establishment of their nature and mutual relation-

* Obtainable from essential oil of valerian, fermented potato-oil, &c.

ship, constitutes the great chemical advance of the last dozen years or so; and, at the present time, a proper understanding of these types enables us to give at once a more or less satisfactory interpretation of even the most recondite discoveries of modern organic chemistry.

(6.) I need scarcely remind you that among the infinite number of bodies known to chemists, some of them, so far as our present knowledge goes, appear to consist of one kind of matter only. For instance, while cinnabar may be proved to consist of two different kinds of matter, known as sulphur and mercury respectively, out of mercury we can obtain nothing but mercury, and out of sulphur nothing but sulphur. Bodies of this description, therefore, which the chemist has not succeeded in resolving into two or more different kinds of matter, are assumed to consist of one kind of matter only, and are accordingly termed simple bodies or elements. These elements amount to about sixty in number, and are possessed of very diverse properties. About four-fifths of them are metallic, as mercury, and silver, and gold, and copper, and lead, and iron. The remainder are non-metallic, as oxygen, and chlorine, and bromine, and sulphur, and phosphorus, and charcoal. The great majority of them exist naturally in the solid state. Only two are liquid, namely, bromine and mercury; while four of them are gaseous, namely, hydrogen, chlorine, oxygen, and nitrogen. Now it is the combinations of these four gaseous elements with one another, or rather, I should say, the combinations of hydrogen with the other three gaseous elements, which constitute our primary chemical types—chloride of hydrogen or hydrochloric acid, oxide of hydrogen or water, and nitride of hydrogen or ammonia—which we will now consider seriatim.

(7.) If we expose a mixture of chlorine and hydrogen gases to diffused daylight, they gradually combine with each other to produce a compound gas called **hydrochloric acid**—the gas which is contained in this sealed tube, and which I dare say I shall be able to render evident to you by breaking off the point of tube under water. The existence of hydrochloric acid gas within the tube is now manifested to you by its complete solution in the water, and by its action upon colouring matter. But, if instead of allowing the two gases to act upon one another slowly in diffused daylight, we expose them to direct sunlight, or if we bring them into contact with flame, their combination then takes place, as you see, instantaneously and with explosion. Now, it has been shown over and over again, that when chlorine and hydrogen gases unite with one another to form hydrochloric acid, it is always in the ratio of equal volumes. If we take one volume of hydrogen and one volume and a quarter of chlorine, the one volume of hydrogen unites with one volume of chlorine, and leaves the extra quarter volume of chlorine unacted upon. In the same way, if we mix together one volume of chlorine and one volume and a quarter of hydrogen, the one volume of chlorine unites with exactly one volume of hydrogen to form hydrochloric acid, leaving the extra quarter volume of hydrogen unacted upon. Try the experiment how we please, we come to the same conclusion, that chlorine and hydrogen gases will unite only in the proportion of volume to volume. But chlorine is exactly 35·5 times heavier than hydrogen; or, taking the specific gravity of hydrogen as unity, the specific gravity of chlorine will be 35·5; or, if we call the weight of a litre of hydrogen 1 crith, the weight of a litre of chlorine will be 35·5 criths. Accordingly, in hydrochloric acid gas we have one volume of hydrogen united with one volume of chlorine, or 1 part by weight of hydrogen united with 35·5 parts by weight of chlorine, thus:—

Hydrochloric acid

| 1 | 35·5 |

Moreover, when hydrogen and chlorine gases unite with one another to form hydrochloric acid gas, they undergo no alteration whatever in bulk. If we take, for instance, a litre of hydrogen and a litre of chlorine, we obtain exactly two litres of hydrochloric acid. This persistence in bulk is capable of being shown by direct experiment, but may be inferred with equal certainty by merely taking the specific gravity of hydrochloric acid gas. The weight of two litres of hydrochloric acid gas, for instance, proving to be identical with the weight of one litre of chlorine, plus that of one litre of hydrogen, it is evident that mixed hydrogen and chlorine on becoming combined hydrogen and chlorine occupy precisely the same bulk before and after combination.

(8.) Turning our attention next to the combination of hydrogen with oxygen, we find that when oxygen and hydrogen gases unite with one another to form water, it is always in the proportion of one volume of oxygen to two volumes of hydrogen; and, conversely, when we decompose water electrolytically into its constituent gases, we find that for every single volume of oxygen liberated at the one pole, we have two volumes of hydrogen liberated at the other. Experiment has proved over and over again that just as chlorine and hydrogen will unite with one another only in the proportion of volume to volume, oxygen and hydrogen will unite with one another only in the proportion of one volume of the former to two volumes of the latter gas. But oxygen is found to be exactly 16 times heavier than hydrogen; or, taking the specific gravity of hydrogen as unity, the specific gravity of oxygen will be 16; or, calling the weight of a litre of hydrogen 1 crith, the weight of a litre of oxygen will be 16 criths. Hence, in water we have two volumes of hydrogen united with one volume of oxygen, or 2 parts by weight of hydrogen united with 16 parts by weight of oxygen, thus:—

Water

When, however, two volumes of hydrogen unite with one volume of oxygen, they do not form three volumes, but only two volumes of gaseous water or steam. That is to say, the three volumes of mixed hydrogen and oxygen form only two volumes of combined hydrogen and oxygen. This condensation is capable of being shown by direct experiment, but really we do not require any such experiment, since the result may be demonstrated with equal certainty by observing the specific gravity of steam. We find, for instance, that the weight of two litres of steam is identical with the conjoint weight of one litre of oxygen and of two litres of hydrogen; so that while from two litres of hydrochloric acid gas we can extract only one litre of hydrogen in addition to the one litre of chlorine, from the same bulk of steam or gaseous water we can extract two litres of hydrogen in addition to the one litre of oxygen. In the experiment taking place on the table of the electrolytic decomposition of water, you see we have roughly, for the single volume of oxygen, a double volume of hydrogen; and by performing the experiment with certain precautions, we should obtain exactly twice as much hydrogen in the one tube as we obtained oxygen in the other.

(9.) Let us now direct our attention to the third typical hydride, namely, hydride of nitrogen or ammonia. The combination of hydrogen with nitrogen to form ammonia can be effected by indirect methods only; but it may be shown by a variety of processes, with which I will not trouble you, that these two gases always unite with each other in the ratio of one volume of nitrogen to three volumes of hydrogen. But nitrogen is found to be exactly 14 times heavier than hydrogen; and, accordingly, taking the specific gravity of hydrogen as unity, the specific gravity of nitrogen will be 14; or, calling the weight of a litre of hydrogen 1 crith, the weight of a litre of nitrogen will be 14 criths. Hence we have in ammonia three volumes of hydrogen combined with one volume of nitrogen, or 3 parts by weight of hydrogen combined with 14 parts by weight of nitrogen, thus:—

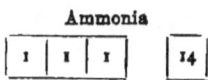

Further, when one volume of nitrogen combines with three volumes of hydrogen to form ammonia, the four volumes become condensed into exactly two volumes. I cannot show you this conversion of four volumes of mixed nitrogen and hydrogen into two volumes of combined nitrogen and hydrogen, but the reverse experiment is of very easy performance. Thus, if we submit ammonia gas to the action of the electric spark, it undergoes decomposition into its elementary constituents, as you perceive. We have here two volumes of ammonia gas, which, by the continued action of the electric spark is decomposed into its constituent nitrogen and hydrogen—and the two volumes of ammonia become gradually increased into four volumes of hydrogen and nitrogen, mixed in the proportion of three volumes of the former to one volume of the latter gas. But in this case, as in the previous two, the information afforded by a determination of the specific gravity of ammonia renders a direct experiment of any kind unnecessary. We find that the weight of two litres of ammonia gas, for instance, is identical with the conjoint weight of one litre of nitrogen and of three litres of hydrogen; so that while from two litres of hydrochloric acid gas we can extract one litre of hydrogen, and from two litres of steam we can extract two litres of hydrogen, so from two litres of ammonia we can extract three litres of hydrogen, in addition to the one litre of chlorine, oxygen, and nitrogen respectively. Or from double volumes of chloride of hydrogen, oxide of hydrogen, and nitride of hydrogen, we may obtain one volume of hydrogen, two volumes of hydrogen, and three volumes of hydrogen respectively, in addition, in each case, to the one volume of chlorine, the one volume of oxygen, and the one volume of nitrogen, as illustrated by these models.

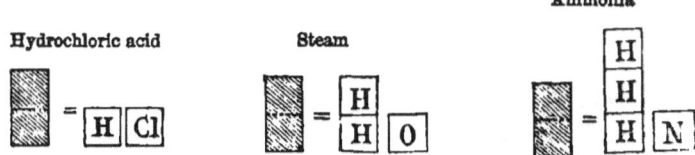

(10.) You will observe that all I have hitherto said with regard to these three hydrides is simply a matter of experiment or observation, uncontrolled by any theory whatever. It is a matter of fact that if we take equal volumes of hydrochloric acid, steam, and ammonia gases, we can extract from the ammonia three times as much hydrogen, and from the steam twice as much hydrogen, as can be got from the hydrochloric acid; whereas the amount of nitrogen we can extract from the ammonia is exactly equal in bulk to the amount of oxygen we can extract from the steam, and to the amount of chlorine, and, consequently, of hydrogen, we can extract from the hydrochloric acid. It is also a matter of fact that taking equal volumes of hydrogen, chlorine, oxygen, and nitrogen, the weights of these equal volumes are in the proportion of

$$1 \;:\; 35\cdot5 \;:\; 16 \;:\; 14$$

as shown more fully in the table before you.

Specific gravities or weights of one volume		Molecules or weights of two volumes	
H	1	H_2	2
Cl	35·5	Cl_2	71
O	16	O_2	32
N	14	N_2	28
$\frac{1}{2}$HCl	18·25	HCl	36·5
$\frac{1}{2}H_2O$	9	H_2O	18
$\frac{1}{2}H_3N$	8·5	H_3N	17
$\frac{1}{2}H_4C$	8	H_4C	16

(11.) Now we come to a matter of interpretation. From these, in addition to many other considerations, we accord to hydrogen, chlorine, oxygen, and nitrogen the atomic weights 1, 35·5, 16, and 14, and we express the comparable molecules of hydrochloric acid, water, and ammonia by the formulæ HCl, H_2O, and H_3N respectively, each of which represents the same gaseous bulk, or 2-volumes of its particular compound. This formula for water is warranted by a host of considerations. It may suffice here to remark that in composition, condensation, and properties, water H_2O, is strictly intermediate between the acid monhydride of chlorine HCl, and the alkaline trihydride of nitrogen H_3N. Further, what is true of hydrochloric acid is also true of hydrofluoric acid, hydrobromic acid, and hydriodic acid. From 2-volumes of each of these gases we are able to extract a single volume of hydrogen; while from equal bulks of sulphuretted, selenetted, and telluretted hydrogen, we are able to extract twice the volume of hydrogen, and from equal bulks of phosphoretted, arsenetted, and antimonetted hydrogen we are able to extract three times the volume of hydrogen that can be got from the same bulk of hydrochloric acid, as indicated in the table.

Monhydrides	Dihydrides	Trihydrides
HF	H_2O	H_3N
HCl	H_2S	H_3P
HBr	H_2Se	H_3As
HI	H_2Te	H_3Sb

(12.) We find, moreover, that chlorine is capable not only of uniting with hydrogen in the proportion of volume to volume, but also of replacing hydrogen in the same ratio in a great variety of compounds. Indeed, we may consider the comparable molecules of free chlorine ClCl, and of hydrochloric acid HCl, to be derived from the molecule of free hydrogen HH, by a displacement of two atoms, and of one atom, of hydrogen respectively, by equivalent quantities of chlorine. Accordingly we are acquainted with chlorides corresponding to all the pre-considered hydrides, ClCl and ClI corresponding to HCl and HI; Cl_2O and Cl_2S corresponding to H_2O and H_2S; and Cl_3N and Cl_3P corresponding to H_3N and H_3P, &c.; and these chlorides when in the gaseous state are found to have exactly the same bulk as their corresponding hydrides. Thus, from two litres of oxide of chlorine Cl_2O, we are able to extract one litre of oxygen and two litres of chlorine, just as from two litres of oxide of hydrogen H_2O, we are able to extract one litre of oxygen and two litres of hydrogen.

Monochlorides	Dichlorides	Trichlorides
ClCl	Cl_2O	Cl_3N
ClI	Cl_2S	Cl_3P
ClNa	Cl_2Zn	Cl_3Al
ClK	Cl_2Ca	Cl_3Au
ClAg	Cl_2Hg	Cl_3Bi

(13.) The metals do not, as a rule, combine with hydrogen, but their chlorides, as shown in the above table, may be divided into three classes, corresponding to the chlorides of the non-metals, by having regard to such considerations as the following: —We find that the proportions of the solid non-metals, iodine, sulphur, and phosphorus, which unite with one, two, and three volumes of hydrogen respectively, and with one, two, and three volumes of chlorine, as shown in the previous tables, and which we have agreed to regard as atomic proportions, have their several specific heats expressed approximately by the number 6·3. Now, if we take for the atomic proportions of the different metals those quantities of each of them which have substantially the same specific heat as one another and as the atomic proportions of the solid non-metals, then we find that the chlorides of the metals, like those of the non-metals, must also be divided into monochlorides, di-chlorides, and trichlorides, &c. Accordingly, we have in the opposite table a list of chlorides of metallic and hydrides of non-metallic elements corresponding, you perceive, with one another.

(14.) Only a few of these metallic chlorides can be vaporised at manageable temperatures; but with regard to such of them as are moderately volatile, it is found that two litres of their several vapours contain as many litres of chlorine as are indicated by their respective formulæ, deduced from the specific heats of their constituent metals. With regard to corrosive sublimate vapour, for instance, we find that from two litres of gaseous chloride of mercury Cl_2Hg, we can extract two litres of chlorine, just as we can from the same bulk of chloride of oxygen Cl_2O; whereas, if we take two litres of chloride of bismuth Cl_3Bi, we can extract therefrom three litres of chlorine, just as we can also extract three litres of chlorine from two litres of chloride of phosphorus Cl_3P. We find, then, that in the case of those metallic chlorides which are volatilisable, we can get from 2-volumes of their respective vapours, quantities of chlorine identical with the quantities obtainable from similarly formulated non-metallic chlorides. I may take the opportunity of saying that from considerations of this sort, together with others of almost equal cogency, it is demonstrable that the formula for corrosive sublimate, $HgCl_2$, in the old 'London Pharmacopœia' is right, while that in the new

FORMULÆ OF METALLIC CHLORIDES. 15

Elements	Atomic weights	Specific heats of atomic weights	Formulæ of chlorides, &c.
Monads—			
Bromine	80	6·74	HBr
Iodine	127	6·87	HI
Lithium	7	6·58	ClL
Sodium	23	6·75	ClNa
Potassium	39	6·61	ClK
Silver	108	6·15	ClAg
Dyads—			
Sulphur	32	5·68	H_2S
Selenium	79·5	6·65	H_2Se
Tellurium	129	6·11	H_2Te
Manganese	55	6·69	Cl_2Mn
Iron	56	6·37	Cl_2Fe
Cobalt	59	6·31	Cl_2Co
Nickel	59	6·41	Cl_2Ni
Copper	63·5	6·04	Cl_2Cu
Magnesium	24	5·99	Cl_2Mg
Zinc	65	6·26	Cl_2Zn
Cadmium	112	6·35	Cl_2Cd
Mercury	200	6·38	Cl_2Hg
Triads—			
Phosphorus	31	5·85	H_3P
Arsenic	75	6·10	H_3As
Antimony	122	6·19	H_3Sb
Bismuth	210	6·47	Cl_3Bi
Aluminum	27·5	5·87	Cl_3Al
Thallium	203	6·81	Cl_3Tl
Gold	196·5	6·37	Cl_3Au
Tetrads—			
Tin	118	6·63	Cl_4Sn
Lead	207	6·50	Et_4Pb
Palladium	106·5	6·31	Cl_4Pd
Platinum	197	6·39	Cl_4Pt

'British Pharmacopæia,' $HgCl$,* is indisputably wrong. In the present state of knowledge, the matter no longer admits of any question whatever.

(15.) Having thus considered our primary hydrides of chlorine, oxygen, and nitrogen, as typical of monad, dyad, and triad combinations in general, I now wish to direct your attention, lastly, to their mutual relationship. Here we have them written up in a convenient form :—

Chlorides	Hydrates	Amides
HCl	$H(HO)$	$H(H_2N)$
KCl	$K(HO)$	$K(H_2N)$
$ZnCl_2$	$Zn(HO)_2$	$Zn(H_2N)_2$
PCl_3	$P(HO)_3$	$P(H_2N)_3$

If under suitable conditions we act upon hydrochloric acid HCl, water $H.HO$, and ammonia $H.H_2N$, by a metal—say by potassium—we obtain in each instance the same reaction. The one atom of potassium turns out one atom of hydrogen; and from each of the three molecules, instead of chloride, oxide, and nitride of hydrogen, we get the chloride, hydrate, and amide of potassium, which may be regarded as compounds of potassium K, with the residues or radicles chlorine Cl, eurhyzen HO, and amidogen H_2N. Hence, caustic potash and potassamide may be regarded as the hydrated and ammoniated forms of chloride of potassium; and in a similar manner, to nearly every chloride, mineral or organic, simple or compound, there exists a corresponding hydrate and amide bearing to it the same relation that caustic potash and potassamide respectively bear to chloride of potassium. If we consider chloride of potassium, for instance, as a compound of metallic potassium, with the residue from hydrochloric

---

* Hg; atomic weight, 200; atomic heat, 6·38 : Hg; atomic weight, 100; atomic heat, 3·19, or half that of the other elements. So that in undergoing an equal increment or decrement of temperature, 200 parts of mercury absorb or evolve the same, and 100 parts of mercury only half the amount of heat absorbed or evolved by 23 parts of sodium, 65 parts of zinc, 108 parts of silver, 210 parts of bismuth, &c.

acid, we can in the same way consider caustic potash as a compound of the metal with the residue from water, and potassamide as a compound of the metal with the residue from ammonia; and hereafter it will appear that some of the most complicated products of tissue metamorphosis are but the ammoniated forms of comparatively simple bodies, just as potassamide is the ammoniated form, and caustic potash the hydrated form, of chloride of potassium. Again, if in chloride of zinc $ZnCl_2$, we replace the two atoms of chlorine by eurhyzen or peroxide of hydrogen, we obtain hydrate of zinc; whereas if we replace them by amidogen we obtain zincamide, as also shown in the above table. Similarly if in chloride of phosphorus PCl_3, we replace the three atoms of chlorine by peroxide of hydrogen, we obtain phosphorous acid; whereas if we replace them by amidogen we obtain phosphoramide; these three bodies being, so to speak, the phosphorus representatives of hydrochloric acid, water, and ammonia, or of chloride of potassium, caustic potash and potassamide.

(16.) Passing on to organic compounds, marsh gas is found to consist of one atom of carbon united with four atoms of hydrogen, so as to constitute the fourth or tetrad term of our series of typical hydrides. Now, if we take the chlorine derivative of this marsh gas—that is, if instead of CH_4 we take CH_3Cl.—and replace the atom of chlorine by an atom of peroxide of hydrogen, we obtain ordinary wood-spirit, whereas if we replace it by amidogen, we obtain **methylamine**, a very common product of the putrefactive decomposition of animal matter, as formulated in the first line of the next table:—

Chlorides	Hydrates	Amides
$C\ H_3Cl$	$C\ H_3(HO)$	$C\ H_3(H_2N)$
$C\ O\ Cl_2$	$C\ O\ (HO)_2$	$C\ O\ (H_2N)_2$
$C_3N_3Cl_3$	$C_3N_3(HO)_3$	$C_3N_3(H_2N)_3$
$C_2H_3ClO_2$	$C_2H_3(HO)O_2$	$C_2H_3(H_2N)O_2$
$C_2H_5ClSO_3$	$C_2H_5(HO)SO_3$	$C_2H_5(H_2N)SO_3$

Again, if in phosgene gas $COCl_2$, we replace the two atoms of chlorine by peroxide of hydrogen, we obtain carbonic acid;

whereas if we replace them by amidogen we get urea, as shown in the second line of the table. Physiologists regard urea as a complex organic body altogether *sui generis*. The chemist regards it merely as the ammoniated form of one of the simplest mineral acids; for the relation of phosgene and carbonic acid to urea is identical with that of hydrochloric acid and water to ammonia, and with that of chloride of potassium and caustic potash to potassamide. Proceeding a little further, if in cyanuric chloride $C_3N_3Cl_3$, we replace the three atoms of chlorine by three atoms of peroxide of hydrogen, we get cyanuric or pyrouric acid; whereas if we replace them by amidogen, we get melamine, a product of the action of heat upon urea. Passing on to chloracetic acid $C_2H_3ClO_2$—a derivative of common acetic acid $C_2H_4O_2$, by the substitution of an atom of chlorine for hydrogen—if in this body we replace the chlorine by peroxide of hydrogen, we obtain glycolic acid; whereas if we replace it by amidogen, we obtain glycocine, or sugar of gelatin, glycocine being only an ammoniated form of the glycolic and chloracetic acids.

The next formula, $C_2H_5ClSO_3$, represents chlorethyl-sulphurous acid, and if in this body we replace the atom of chlorine by an atom of peroxide of hydrogen, we obtain isethionic acid; whilst if we replace it by amidogen, we obtain a compound of which I have already spoken, namely, taurine,—taurine, isethionic acid, and chlorethyl-sulphurous acid being respectively the amidated, hydrated, and chlorinated forms of one and the same body, being, in fact, ethyl-sulphurous varieties of hydrochloric acid, water, and ammonia.

(17.) You perceive that this establishment between most complicated and diverse bodies of relations similar to those subsisting between hydrochloric acid, water, and ammonia—between chloride of potassium, caustic potash, and potassamide—furnishes us with a key to the composition and metamorphoses of a whole host of organic compounds; but the generalisation is capable of being pushed much farther. In bodies with two atoms of chlorine, we may replace either one or both of them by eurhyzen, or by amidogen; or we may replace one of them by eurhyzen and the other by amidogen; whilst in bodies containing three or four atoms of chlorine, the possible number of derived bodies increases in a very rapid manner, according to the ordinary algebraic rule of combinations. I have here written down the names of a few well-known double chloro-hydrates, chloro-amides, and hydrate-amides, by way of illustration.

Mixed Hydrate-Amides, &c.

CuF_2	Cupric difluoride
$CuF.HO$	Cupric fluorhydrate
$HgCl_2$	Mercuric dichloride
$HgCl.H_2N$	Mercuric chloramide
$C_3N_3.Cl_3$	Cyanuric trichloride
$C_3N_3.Cl(H_2N)_2$	Cyanuric chloro-diamide
$C_3N_3(HO)_3$	Cyanuric trihydrate
$C_3N_3(HO)_2(H_2N)$	Cyanuric dihydrate-amide
$C_3N_3(HO)(H_2N)_2$	Cyanuric hydrate-diamide
$C_3N_3(H_2N)_3$	Cyanuric triamide

First of all we have difluoride of copper, or cupric difluoride, followed by cupric fluorhydrate. Next we have mercuric dichloride or corrosive sublimate, and then mercuric chloramide, or white precipitate, a body in which one of the original chlorine atoms is replaced by amidogen. Next we come to cyanuric trichloride and its numerous derivatives, in the first of which, namely, cyanuric chloro-diamide, two of the original chlorine atoms are replaced by amidogen. Then we have in succession cyanuric trihydrate or ordinary pyro-uric acid, cyanuric dihydrate-amide or melanuric acid, cyanuric hydrate-diamide or ammeline, and lastly cyanuric triamide or melamine, a body produced, as I have already said, by the action of heat upon urea.

(18.) Let me give you one more illustration of this relationship. I have said that urea CH_4N_2O, is an ammoniated form of carbonic acid; but we are acquainted with another urinary product, namely, guanidine CH_5N_3, which is an ammoniated form of urea, and accordingly bears to urea much the same relation that urea itself bears to carbonic acid, thus:—

$CN_2H_3(HO)$ Urea
$CN_2H_3(H_2N)$ Guanidine

I refrain, for the present, from entering into further details upon this subject. I have shown the wide applicability of the generalisation, and that by its means we are capable of associating with one another the most diverse bodies, and of establishing between them the same simple relations which subsist between hydrochloric acid, water, and ammonia; and in particular I have pointed out that some of the best known products of tissue metamorphosis are in reality only the ammoniated forms of comparatively simple bodies. In my next lecture I shall endeavour to satisfy you that the complex character of many organic bodies is more apparent than real, and that most of them may be resolved into comparatively simple molecules, which are capable of being distributed into certain well defined groups and series; and I shall take, as concrete illustrations of the point I wish to establish, the composition of salicin among vegetable, and that of hippuric acid among animal products.

LECTURE II.

Proximate animal and vegetable principles included in the class of organic compounds, together with various bodies resulting from their natural and artificial metamorphoses—Carbon the characteristic element of organic compounds—Number, variety, and complexity of its combinations with hydrogen and oxygen—Highly complex organic bodies built up of less complex molecules—Salicin formed of saligenin and glucose; populin of benzoic acid, saligenin, and glucose—Occurrence of constituent molecules in an incomplete state—Doctrine of residues—Existence of minute residues of acetic acid and ammonia in aceto-nitrile, and of oxalic acid and ammonia in cyanogen—Residues of constituent molecules ever ready to regenerate complete and separate molecules by an absorption of water—Aplone molecules either possessed of simple constitution, or associated with bodies of simple constitution as members of the same family—Distribution of aplone molecules into series of similarly constituted compounds—Also into groups of dissimilarly constituted compounds susceptible of mutual metamorphosis—Series of primary fatty acids—Propionic and butyric groups—Relations of alcohols and glycols to mono- and di-basic acids—Nature of homologous series—Differences and resemblances between the fatty acids—Series of aromatic acids and hydrocarbons—Other groups and series—Every aplone molecule referrible to a definite position in some homologous series and heterologous grouping—Hippuric acid formed of three constituent residues, convertible into complete molecules by an absorption of water—Assignment of these molecules to appropriate positions in groups and series—Possibility of obtaining any two residues in combination, by destruction or removal of third—Assumed pre-existence of benzamide, benzoglycolic acid, and glycocine in hippuric acid—Probable internal arrangement of the acid—Illustrative animal products formed of two constituent residues—Urea, glycocine, leucine—Analogy of spermaceti and myricin to acetic ether—The true fats—Illustrative animal products formed of more than two residues—Taurine, sarcosine, alloxan, and the biliary acids—Scheme of the constitution of kreatine.

(19.) CHEMISTS have ascertained that the various tissues of plants and animals are composed of, or contain, a great number of distinct chemical compounds, capable, for the most part, of being separated from one another by what may be regarded as physical processes—that is to say, by processes dependent on differences of volatility, fusibility, solubility in different menstrua, &c. These several compounds have either been built up in the living plant or animal, or been formed spontaneously in the dead plant or animal out of ancestral substances which were themselves built up in the living plant or animal. Somehow or other these proximate animal and vegetable principles, as they are termed, have been produced through the agency of vitality. They have been formed through the intervention of living organisms, and are hence called organic compounds, in contradistinction to such substances as quartz and feldspar and hæmatite, which pre-exist in the mineral kingdom, and from such substances as copperas and alum and carbonate of soda, which are produced artificially by human ingenuity out of the pre-existing compounds of the mineral kingdom.

(20.) When the chemist gets hold of these different tissue products and components he submits them to a variety of experiments, and subjects them to the most strange transformations; he performs a simple subtraction, by taking away certain constituent atoms and leaving the remainder; or he performs a simple addition, by affixing other constituent atoms, whether of the same or a different nature; or he performs a substitution, taking away certain constituent atoms and introducing fresh ones in their places; or he effects a more or less complete decomposition, by breaking up the original substance into a variety of less complex bodies. Now, all these products into which the chemist transforms the proximate vegetable and animal principles, of which we have spoken, belong to the class of organic compounds. As a rule, they do not pre-exist in living organisms, they are not formed spontaneously in dead organisms, but they result from the skill of the chemist operating upon compounds which were

ORGANIC OR CARBON COMPOUNDS. 23

formed at some time or other through the agency of living organisms. Just as alum and carbonate of soda, which the chemist manufactures out of native minerals, belong to the class of mineral compounds, so do such substances as chloroform and aniline and cyanuric acid, which the chemist manufactures out of the proximate principles of plants and animals, belong to the class of organic compounds.

(21.) It is found that all organic compounds, whether of natural or artificial production, contain carbon as an essential constituent; nearly all of them contain hydrogen also; while the great majority consist of carbon, hydrogen, and oxygen. In my last lecture I brought under your notice certain nitrogenous products of tissue metamorphosis, but confining our present attention to such organic bodies as consist of carbon, hydrogen, and oxygen, or of carbon and hydrogen only, I would speak to you, in the first place, of their immense number and variety. If we take any three elements whatsoever, exclusive of carbon, we shall find that by their mutual combination they very rarely indeed form more than half-a-dozen definite and distinct compounds; but we are acquainted with some thousands of compounds composed solely of carbon, hydrogen, and oxygen united with one another in different quantities and proportions; which thousands of compounds differ most strikingly in their properties, but were all produced originally in living organisms, or made artificially by a transformation of antecedent compounds produced originally in living organisms.

(22.) In addition to their number and variety, organic or carbon compounds are characterised by the complexity of their constitution; that is, by the number of constituent atoms of which their respective molecules are composed. If we take any definite mineral substance containing only three different kinds of elementary matter, corresponding to the carbon, hydrogen, and oxygen of the bodies now under consideration, we shall find that the number of constituent atoms in such mineral substance very rarely indeed exceeds ten or twelve, never perhaps reaches twenty; whereas, among organic or carbon compounds, bodies containing scores of constituent atoms are very frequently met with, a few of which, by way of illustration, are written up on the table before you.

Formulæ	Proximate Organic Principles	Atoms
$C_6H_{10}O_5$	Starch	21
$C_6H_{14}O_6$	Mannite	26
$C_{13}H_{18}O_7$	Salicin	38
$C_{20}H_{22}O_8$	Populin	50
$C_{27}H_{22}O_{17}$	Tannin	66
$C_{26}H_{44}O$	Cholesterin	71
$C_{32}H_{64}O_2$	Spermaceti	98
$C_{46}H_{92}O_2$	Myricin	140
$C_{57}H_{110}O_6$	Stearin	173

First of all we have starch, a compound consisting of 6 atoms of carbon, 10 of hydrogen, and 5 of oxygen, making altogether 21 atoms. Next we have mannite, the crystallisable principle of ordinary manna, of which it forms, I believe, as much as 60 or 70 per cent. It contains, as shown by its formula, 6 atoms of carbon, 14 of hydrogen, and 6 of oxygen, making altogether 26 atoms. Next we come to the crystallisable bitter principle of willow bark, namely, salicin, which, I am informed by manufacturers, is still largely produced and used as a substitute for quinine. It is characterised, as you see, by the red colouration it experiences when acted upon by sulphuric acid, and consists, as shown by its formula, of 38 constituent atoms. Next we come to populin, a similar crystallisable principle, less generally known and less widely distributed. It is found in the bark and leaves of the poplar, and contains 50 constituent atoms; while tannin contains 66 atoms, and cholesterin 71. I may take this opportunity of observing that cholesterin, heretofore regarded as an exclusively animal product, is now known to enjoy an extensive distribution in the vegetable kingdom, having been extracted from peas, wheat, almond oil, olive oil, &c. We pass on to spermaceti, with its 98 atoms; to myricin, or purified beeswax, with its 140 atoms; and, lastly, to stearin, with its 173 atoms of carbon, hydrogen, and oxygen. Comparing tri-elementary bodies of this kind with tri-elementary mineral substances in which the number of atoms seldom exceeds 10 or 12, you perceive that the compounds presented for our consideration appear at the first glance to be possessed of a highly complicated nature.

(23.) But in the majority of instances a minute chemical examination of these apparently complex organic bodies has led to the conclusion that they are formed, if I may so say, by the agglomeration of certain less complex molecules. Taking salicin and populin as illustrations, we find that salicin readily breaks up into the less complex molecules known as saligenin and glucose or grape sugar, while populin breaks up into a molecule of saligenin, a molecule of grape-sugar, and a molecule of benzoic acid. I have here a specimen of saligenin or salicylic alcohol, a beautiful crystalline body, which even when in very weak solution is capable of being recognised by its action on perchloride of iron. Thus, on adding tincture of iron to a dilute solution of saligenin, we get a deep purple colour developed by the mutual reaction of the two bodies, as you observe. Salicin, then, by an absorption of water, breaks up into the less complex bodies saligenin and glucose, as shown in this equation,—

$$\underset{\text{Salicin}}{C_{13}H_{18}O_7} + \underset{\text{Water}}{H_2O} = \underset{\text{Saligenin}}{C_7H_8O_2} + \underset{\text{Glucose}}{C_6H_{12}O_6};$$

while, under similar circumstances, populin, with its 50 constituent atoms, breaks up into saligenin, glucose, and benzoic acid, thus :—

$$\underset{\text{Populin}}{C_{20}H_{22}O_8} + \underset{\text{Water}}{2H_2O} = \underset{\text{Saligenin}}{C_7H_8O_2} + \underset{\text{Glucose}}{C_6H_{12}O_6} + \underset{\text{Benzoic acid}}{C_7H_6O_2}$$

(24.) Confining our attention to salicin, the point I wish to impress upon you in relation to this body is, that it does not really contain either saligenin or glucose in the state of a complete molecule. Adding together the number of atoms of carbon, hydrogen, and oxygen in saligenin, and the number of atoms of the same elements in glucose, we find they are in excess of the number of atoms contained in the molecule of salicin, as shown in this table.

1 Saligenin	$C_7H_8O_4$	1 Salicin	$C_{13}H_{18}O_7$
1 Glucose	$C_6H_{12}O_6$	1 Water	H_2O
	$C_{13}H_{20}O_8$		$C_{13}H_{20}O_8$

Hence the necessity for the atom of water, which has to be incorporated by the salicin before it can split up into its constituents. We may say, then, that salicin does not contain either saligenin or glucose as such, but that it contains, in a state of combination, a residue of saligenin and a residue of glucose, which are, as it were, ever on the alert to take up water, and so produce the separate and distinct molecules, saligenin and glucose respectively. If we attempted to represent the composition of salicin graphically, we should not place two complete circles in apposition side by side, thus,—

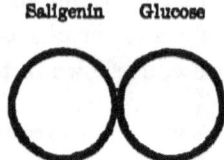

but we should place two incomplete circles, or the residues of two circles, in conjunction, thus :—

(25.) Similarly, with regard to populin, it does not actually contain saligenin, glucose, and benzoic acid, but is made up of the residues of these three bodies, which can only be obtained in their complete and separate state by an incorporation of the elements of water with the populin, thus :—

1 Saligenin	$C_7H_8O_2$	1 Populin		$C_{20}H_{22}O_8$
1 Glucose	$C_6H_{12}O_6$	2 Water		H_4O_2
1 Benzoic acid	$C_7H_6O_2$			
	$C_{20}H_{26}O_{10}$			$C_{20}H_{26}O_{10}$

Accordingly, we should not represent populin graphically by three complete circles in apposition, but by the residues of three circles conjoined with one another, as in one or other of these figures:—

Populin

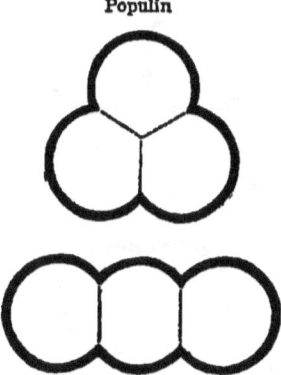

(26.) The constituent residues existing in salicin and populin form very considerable proportions of the original molecules but in many instances the residues become extremely small. For instance, by combining acetic acid with ammonia we obtain acetate of ammonia, a salt produced by the direct union of the two complete molecules, acetic acid and ammonia. Under certain circumstances an atom of water may be eliminated from this acetate of ammonia, whereby it becomes converted into acetamide, which by further loss of an atom of water becomes acetonitrile, as shown in the following diagrams.

Thus, in acetamide the residues of acetic acid and ammonia constitute but 59 out of 77 parts, while in aceto-nitrile they amount to only 41 parts, or little more than half the weight of the original molecule. Nevertheless, in aceto-nitrile the two small residues stand apart from one another as perfect representatives of, or proxies for, the entire molecules, ready without a moment's notice to regenerate them on the concurrence of suitable conditions.

Under a variety of circumstances both acetamide and acetonitrile absorb the elements of water, with reconversion into acetate of ammonia, a body containing the complete antagonistic molecules, to which the constituent residues of the amide and nitrile alike appertain.

Acetat-ammonia	$C_2H_4O_4$	+	H_3N			=	$C_2H_7NO_4$
	60	+	17	–	0	=	77

Acet-amide	$C_2H_4O_4$	+	H_3N	–	H_2O	=	C_2H_5NO
	60	+	17	–	18	=	59

Aceto-nitrile	$C_2H_4O_2$	+	H_3N	–	$2H_2O$	=	C_2H_3N
	60	+	17	–	36	=	41

(27). Let me give you one additional illustration of this doctrine of residues. Upon applying a gentle heat to certain metallic cyanides we obtain cyanogen gas, which is recognisable by the beautiful violet-coloured flame with which it burns, as you see, at the mouth of the tube. In this experiment the cyanogen is being made by heating cyanide of silver, but it is capable of being produced in an entirely different manner. For if, instead of combining ammonia with acetic acid, we combine it with oxalic acid, and if from the resulting oxalate of ammonia we abstract water, we thereby obtain cyanogen, as shown in this table:—

CONSTITUENT RESIDUES.

		Formulæ	At. Weights
1	Oxalic acid	$C_2H_2O_4$	90
2	Ammonia (H_3N)	H_6N_2	34
		$C_2H_8N_2O_4$	124
4	Water (H_2O)	$H_8 \quad O_4$	72
1	Cyanogen	$C_2 \quad N_2$	52

The formula for oxalic acid is $C_2H_2O_4$, and its atomic weight 90. With this we combine 2 atoms, or 34 parts by weight, of ammonia, H_6N_2. Adding these together, we get 124 for the atomic weight of oxalate of ammonia. When from this we subtract 4 atoms or 72 parts by weight of water, we have left only 2 atoms of carbon from the oxalic acid, and 2 atoms of nitrogen from the ammonia, which exist united with one another to form a double atom, or single molecule, of cyanogen gas, and amount to only 52 parts out of 124, or to considerably less than half the weight of the original compound. In cyanogen, then, the only evidence of the original oxalic acid is carbon, and the only evidence of the original ammonia is nitrogen. Nevertheless, the constituent carbon and nitrogen of this remarkable gas, which in so many of its properties resembles certain of the elementary bodies, are not incorporated with one another, but remain apart, in the same way as do the residues of saligenin and glucose in salicin, and the residues of acetic acid and ammonia in acetonitrile, thus:—

Cyanogen

Accordingly we find that cyanogen gas, when dissolved in water, gradually absorbs the water necessary to re-form oxalic acid and ammonia, the entire molecules, of which the small residues of carbon and nitrogen are but the representatives. In cyanogen gas, no matter how produced, there is a something, however small, pertaining to oxalic acid, a something, however small, pertaining to ammonia. The residues are not intermingled promiscuously, but remain apart, ever mindful of their distinct individualities, ever longing to re-form the complete and separate molecules from which they sprung.

(28.) The progress of organic chemistry, then, has led to the conclusion that highly complex molecules are built up of the residues of less complex molecules, which constituent residues, by a direct or indirect absorption of water, are capable of separation from one another, and reproduction in their isolated and perfect state. Accordingly, we regard highly complex or polymerone bodies as compounds formed by the union of less complex or aplone bodies with one another, the union being attended by an elimination of water. Now, these aplone molecules, of which our constituent residues represent greater or less portions, are found either to have a very simple constitution, or to be associated with bodies of a very simple constitution, as members of one and the same organic family. Despite their enormous number, the great majority of them have been already referred to certain definite positions in certain very simple groups and series; and we have every reason to believe that, with increase of knowledge, they will all be referred in a similar manner to groups and series, such as these to which I am pointing. Organic chemistry, then, has achieved this great analytic success. The compounds so elaborately built up by living organisms, it has taken to pieces, and the pieces themselves it has arranged into natural series and groups of associated bodies—into series of bodies of similar constitution and similar properties that are not susceptible of mutual metamorphosis, and into groups of bodies of dissimilar constitution and dissimilar properties that are susceptible of mutual metamorphosis.

(29.) Here, for example, we have a series of bodies, namely, the primary monobasic fatty acids, beginning with formic acid CH_2O_2, and ending for the present, at any rate, with melissic acid, $C_{30}H_{60}O_2$. Some of these acids have, as you perceive, a very simple, others a somewhat complex constitution, but all of them present an obvious similarity of constitution, manifest the same general reactions, and are related to one another by a regular gradation, both of properties and composition.

Monatomic Fatty Acid Series

$C\ H_2\ O_2$	Formic	$C_{13}H_{26}O_2$	Cocinic
$C_2\ H_4\ O_2$	*Acetic*	$C_{14}H_{28}O_2$	Myristic
$C_3\ H_6\ O_2$	*Propionic*	$C_{15}H_{30}O_2$	Benic
$C_4\ H_8\ O_2$	*Butyric*	$C_{16}H_{32}O_2$	Palmitic
$C_5\ H_{10}O_2$	Valeric	$C_{17}H_{34}O_2$	Margaric
$C_6\ H_{12}O_2$	Caproic	$C_{18}H_{36}O_2$	Stearic
$C_7\ H_{14}O_2$	Œnanthic	$C_{19}H_{38}O_2$	Balenic
$C_8\ H_{16}O_2$	Thetic	$C_{20}H_{40}O_2$	Arachidic
$C_9\ H_{18}O_2$	Pelargic	$C_{21}H_{42}O_2$	Nardic
$C_{10}H_{20}O_2$	Rutic		
$C_{11}H_{22}O_2$	Enodic	$C_{27}H_{54}O_2$	Cerotic
$C_{12}H_{24}O_2$	Lauric	$C_{30}H_{60}O_2$	Melissic

(30.) But in the succeeding tables we have two of our primary monobasic fatty acids—namely, the third or **propionic acid**, and the fourth or **butyric acid**—associated each with a set of bodies dissimilar to the acid, and dissimilar to one another; but all containing the same number of carbon atoms as the particular acid, and correlated with it and with one another by a susceptibility of mutual metamorphosis, to such an extent indeed, that they may almost be looked upon as varieties of one and the same primitive body.

Propionic Group

$C_3\ H_8$	Propene	$C_3\ H_6$	Propylene
$C_3\ H_8\ O$	Propyl-alcohol	$C_3\ H_6\ O$	Allyl-alcohol
$C_3\ H_8\ O_2$	Propyl-glycol	—	,,
$C_3\ H_8\ O_3$	Glycerin	—	,,
$C_3\ H_6\ O$	Propion-aldehyd	$C_3\ H_4\ O$	Acrolic aldehyd
$C_3\ H_6\ O_2$	*Propionic acid*	$C_3\ H_4\ O_2$	Acrolic acid
$C_3\ H_6\ O_3$	Lactic acid	$C_3\ H_4\ O_3$	Pyruvic acid
$C_3\ H_6\ O_4$	Glyceric acid	—	,,
$C_3\ H_4\ O_4$	Malonic acid	—	,,
$C_3\ H_4\ O_5$	Tartronic acid	$C_3\ H_2\ O_5$	Mesoxalic acid

Butyric Group

C_4H_{10}	Butene	C_4H_8	Butylene
$C_4H_{10}O$	Butyl-alcohol	—	,,
$C_4H_{10}O_2$	Butyl-glycol	—	,,
C_4H_8O	Butyr-aldehyd	—	,,
$C_4H_8O_2$	*Butyric acid*	$C_4H_6O_2$	Crotonic acid
$C_4H_8O_3$	Bulatic acid	—	,,
$C_4H_6O_4$	Succinic acid	$C_4H_4O_4$	Fumaric acid
$C_4H_6O_5$	Malic acid	$C_4H_4O_5$	Metatartric acid
$C_4H_6O_6$	Tartaric acid	—	,,

(31.) Of the correlated bodies comprised in groups of this description, chemists attach far greater importance to those occupying certain particular positions, than to the remainder. Thus, the principal terms of every well represented organic group—such as the propionic, and butyric, to which I have just directed your attention—are, 1st, the monatomic alcohol; 2nd, the monobasic acid corresponding thereto; 3rd, the diatomic alcohol or glycol; and 4th, the dibasic acid corresponding thereto, as shown below in the case of the 2-carbon and 3-carbon groups, for instance:—

Principal Group-Terms

C_2H_6O	Alcohol	C_3H_8O	Propyl-alcohol
$C_2H_4O_2$	*Acetic acid*	$C_3H_6O_2$	*Propionic acid*
$C_2H_6O_2$	Glycol	$C_3H_8O_2$	Propyl-glycol
$C_2H_2O_4$	Oxalic acid	$C_3H_4O_4$	Malonic acid

The monobasic acid, you observe, differs in composition from its correlated alcohol by containing one additional atom of oxygen in place of two subtracted atoms of hydrogen; while the dibasic acid differs from its correlated glycol by containing two additional atoms of oxygen in place of four subtracted atoms of hydrogen. But even of these four principal members of every complete organic group, by far the most importance is attached to the monobasic acid, which is accordingly selected in preference to the alcohol, glycol, or dibasic acid as the characteristic term or pivot of the group. As a rule, the series of monobasic acids is more complete than that of the other terms; the bodies themselves enjoy an extensive natural distribution, either in the isolated condition or in the form of constituent residues; they can be obtained in a comparatively pure state, many of them occurring as commercial products; and their properties, both as individuals and as a class, have been very carefully investigated.

(32.) Nearly all of these primàry monobasic acids are capable of being distributed into one or other of two principal series, known as the fatty and aromatic series respectively. To the fatty acid series, beginning with the formic, acetic, and propionic acids, I have already directed your attention. You observe that each successive member of the series differs in composition from its predecessor by an increment of 1 atom of carbon and 2 atoms of hydrogen. Bodies in which this difference of CH_2 prevails are said to be homologous, and the series of fatty acids is accordingly spoken of as a homologous series. It is noticeable (*vide* preceding table of monatomic fatty acids series) that from the first to the twenty-first term, the series is complete, while between the twenty-first and thirtieth terms only one intermediate acid is known, namely, cerotic acid, an important constituent of ordinary beeswax, and especially of the so-called Chinese wax, secreted by an insect of the coccus tribe. Now, while the difference in composition and properties between the acids at either extremity of this series is very great, that between any two or three consecutive acids, more especially of those low down in the list, is so slight as to be scarcely appreciable. Thus the formic and acetic acids when in a state of purity are perfectly mobile, strongly corrosive liquids; the butyric, valeric, and caproic acids are thin oils; while the palmitic, margaric, and stearic acids are mild inactive solids. In comparing formic with palmitic acid, which is only two-thirds of the way down the list, we scarcely perceive a single point of resemblance; but in comparing formic with acetic acid, or still more decidedly in comparing palmitic acid with the margaric and stearic acids, the difficulty is rather to see the difference than the resemblance between them. Moreover, between even the upper and lower members of the series there is a latent similarity, and indeed certain well-marked properties are common to all the acids under consideration. They are all volatile, inflammable, saponifiable, monobasic, and decomposible in a similar manner under the influence of the same reagents. We are not in the habit of regarding vinegar in any form as an inflammable material, but in reality strong acetic acid is almost as inflammable as alcohol. It only requires to be heated externally for a few minutes, when it burns as you observe with a large, lambent, feebly luminous flame. Neither are we in the habit of regarding the acetates as soaps, yet solutions of acetates possess the property of forming a persistent froth or lather to such an extent as to be highly characteristic; so that by searching out for latent resemblances we can perceive that the different members of the series, from the top to the bottom, are associated with one another in a very intimate manner.

(33.) The primary aromatic acids at present known are far less numerous, and the series consequently is far more limited, as shown in this table:—

Monatomic Aromatic Acid Series

$C_6 H_4 O_2$	Collic ?
$C_7 H_6 O_2$	*Benzoic*
$C_8 H_8 O_2$	Toluic
$C_9 H_{10} O_2$	Picic
$C_{10} H_{12} O_2$	Cuminic

These acids correspond generally with the previously considered fatty acids, in the reactions of which they are susceptible, and in their mutual relationship. The first on the list, or collic acid, is said to result from the artificial oxidation of albuminous matter, but its existence is at any rate open to question. Next we have benzoic acid, which is usually regarded as the representative in the aromatic, of acetic acid in the fatty series. This is followed by two acids of which at present comparatively little is known, namely, the toluic and picic; while the list is terminated by cuminic acid, a product formed by the spontaneous oxidation of the chief constituent of oil of cumin. Now, just as the acetic, propionic, and butyric acids are associated each with their respective hydrocarbons, alcohols, aldehydes, and more highly oxidised acids, as shown in the group-tables to which I have already adverted, so is every other primary monobasic acid, both of the fatty and aromatic series, associated with a more or less complete set of congeners, having to it the same relations of composition, properties, and mutual metamorphosis, that the various members of the acetic, propionic, and butyric families have to the acetic, propionic, and butyric acids respectively. Here, for example, we have tabulated the principal compounds which are associated in this manner with benzoic acid:—

Benzoic Group.

$C_7 H_8$	Benzoene
$C_7 H_8 O$	Benzyl-alcohol
$C_7 H_8 O_2$	Benzyl-glycol
$C_7 H_6 O$	Benz-aldehyd
$C_7 H_6 O_2$	*Benzoic acid*
$C_7 H_6 O_3$	Ampelic acid, &c.

(34.) Conversely, we may select any set of compounds occupying analogous positions in the different groups, and arrange them in series corresponding to those of the monobasic acids. Here, for instance, we have the series of aromatic hydrocarbons:—

Aromatic Hydrocarbon Series

$C_6 H_6$	Phenene
$C_7 H_8$	Benzoene
$C_8 H_{10}$	Xylene
$C_9 H_{12}$	Retinene
$C_{10} H_{14}$	Cymene

Again, in the next table we have the two series of primary fatty alcohols and of aldehydes resulting from their dehydrogenation:—

Fatty Alcohol Series		Fatty Aldehyd Series	
$C H_4 O$	Methylic	$C Cl_2 O$	Chloroformic
$C_2 H_6 O$	Ethylic	$C_2 H_4 O$	Acetic
$C_3 H_8 O$	Propylic	$C_3 H_6 O$	Propionic
$C_4 H_{10} O$	Butylic	$C_4 H_8 O$	Butyric
$C_5 H_{12} O$	Amylic	$C_5 H_{10} O$	Valeric
$C_6 H_{14} O$	Caprylic	$C_6 H_{12} O$	Caproic
$C_7 H_{16} O$	Anthylic	$C_7 H_{14} O$	Œnanthic
	&c.		&c.

Lastly, we have the carbonic and oxalic series of acids appertaining to the primary monobasic acids, and to the above tabulated alcohols and aldehydes:—

Diatomic Fatty Acid Series

$C H_2 O_3$	Carbonic	—	,,
$C_2 H_4 O_3$	Glycolic	$C_2 H_2 O_4$	Oxalic
$C_3 H_6 O_3$	Lactic	$C_3 H_4 O_4$	Malonic
$C_4 H_8 O_3$	Bulatic	$C_4 H_6 O_4$	Succinic
$C_5 H_{10} O_3$	Phocic	$C_5 H_8 O_4$	Pyrotartric
$C_6 H_{12} O_3$	Leucic	$C_6 H_{10} O_4$	Adipic
$C_7 H_{14} O_3$ ⎫		$C_7 H_{12} O_4$	Pimelic
$C_8 H_{16} O_3$ ⎬ Wanting		$C_8 H_{14} O_4$	Suberic
$C_9 H_{18} O_3$ ⎥		$C_9 H_{16} O_4$	Anchoic
$C_{10} H_{20} O_3$ ⎭		$C_{10} H_{18} O_4$	Sebacic

Accordingly, when we break up any complex animal product into its simpler constituent molecules, by an absorption of water, we are always, or nearly always, able to refer each of the completed molecules to its appropriate position in some homologous series and in some heterologous grouping; just as we accord to common ethylic alcohol its proper place both in the series of alcohols and in the group of acetic compounds.

(35.) Now, let us apply these several considerations to unravel the composition and relationship of some particular animal product, say hippuric acid, of which a very beautiful specimen, kindly lent me for the occasion by Messrs. Hopkins and Williams, stands on the table before you. This acid is represented by the very complex formula $C_9H_9NO_3$, and is composed, therefore, of 22 constituent atoms. It is now known to consist of a residue of benzoic acid, a residue of oxiacetic or glycolic acid, and a residue of ammonia, united with one another in a particular manner. The positions of the benzoic and glycolic acids in the groups and series to which they belong have been already referred to—the benzoic being the second term of the primary aromatic acid series, and the glycolic the second term of the carbonic acid series—the former being the pivot of the benzoic, the latter a well known member of the acetic group.

CONSTITUTION OF HIPPURIC ACID. 37

α. Benzoic acid	$C_7H_6\ O_2$
β. Oxiacetic acid	$C_2H_4\ O_3$
γ. Ammonia	H_3N
	$C_9H_{13}NO_5$
− 2 Water	$H_4\ O_2$
Hippuric acid	$C_9H_9\ NO_3$

(36.) You observe that by subtracting two atoms of water from the sum of the atoms of carbon, hydrogen, nitrogen, and oxygen contained in the three molecules of benzoic acid, oxiacetic acid, and ammonia, there is left a compound having the formula of hippuric acid. Now there are few bodies about whose intimate constitution greater varieties of opinion have been maintained than with regard to this acid. Each successive chemist who has submitted it to examination has acted upon it with a different reagent, and accordingly as the special reagent employed has attacked one or other of the different residues entering into its constitution, so has a different hypothetical formula been accorded to the unfortunate body. Of the three constituent residues, the oxiacetic is the most easily oxidisable, and accordingly when hippuric acid is acted upon by oxidising agents, peroxide of lead for instance, the acetic residue is destroyed, while the benzoic and ammonia residues remain combined with one another in the form of benzamide. Hence hippuric acid was represented as a compound of some form of acetic acid with benzamide, which is itself resolvable into benzoic acid and ammonia. (Fehling.)

α. Benzoic acid	$C_7H_6\ O_2$
γ. Ammonia	H_3N
	$C_7H_9NO_2$
− Water	$H_2\ O$
Benzamide	C_7H_7NO

(37.) Ammonia undergoes a very remarkable decomposition when acted upon by nitrous acid, its hydrogen being transformed into water and its nitrogen liberated in the gaseous state, together with the nitrogen of the nitrous acid, thus:—

Ammonia		Nitrous acid		Water		Nitrogen
H_3N	+	HNO_2	=	$2H_2O$	+	N_2

Accordingly, when hippuric acid is treated with nitrous acid, its ammoniacal residue is similarly destroyed by the nitrous acid, while the two other residues are left combined with one another in the form of benzoglycolic acid. Hence, hippuric acid has been represented as a combination of ammonia with benzoglycolic acid, which is itself susceptible of decomposition into its constituent benzoic and glycolic acids. (Strecker.)

α. Benzoic acid	$C_7H_6O_4$
β. Glycolic acid	$C_2H_4O_3$
	$C_9H_{10}O_5$
— Water	H_2O
Benzoglycolic acid	$C_9H_8O_4$

(38.) I am not aware of any reagents capable of destroying the benzoic residue, and so leaving the glycolic and ammoniacal residues in combination with one another; but on boiling hippuric acid with acids or alkalies, the benzoic may be separated from the other two residues, which are thus obtained in the form of glycocine, or sugar of gelatin. Hence hippuric has been, and is now, commonly regarded as a compound of benzoic acid with glycocine, which is itself resolvable into glycolic acid and ammonia. (Dessaignes.)

β. Glycolic acid	$C_2H_4O_3$
γ. Ammonia	H_3N
	$C_2H_7NO_3$
— Water	H_2O
Glycocine	$C_2H_5NO_2$

(39.) Our actual knowledge, then, of the constitution of hippuric acid amounts to this, that it contains the residues of three distinct molecules, which by an absorption of water are capable of being obtained separate from one another. When any one of these residues is destroyed or removed, the other two residues are left in combination; and accordingly by treating hippuric acid with different reagents, we may obtain the benzoic and ammoniacal residues in the form of benzamide, or the benzoic and glycolic residues in the form of benzoglycolic acid, or the glycolic and ammoniacal residues in the form of sugar of gelatin. To this much, which is certain, a something may be added which is probable. From many considerations into which I cannot at present enter, it seems, at any rate, that the ammoniacal constituent of hippuric acid is actually in more intimate association with the glycolic than with the benzoic residue, so that the composition of hippuric acid would be better represented by a chain of three circles than by a trefoil, as contrasted in the diagram below; although, as I have said, the benzoic and ammoniacal residues may be left in combination with one another by the excision, so to speak, of the glycolic or oxiacetic residue.

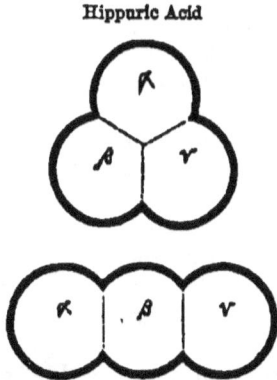

Hippuric Acid

Be this as it may, I shall assume that hippuric acid consists of a residue of benzoic acid and a residue of glycocine, which last consists of a residue of glycolic or oxiacetic acid combined with a residue of ammonia; and similarly in the case of many other bodies composed of more than two ultimate residues, I shall assume, with greater or less warrant, that we *can* ascertain the mode in which the residues are successively appended to one another, as in the second list of bodies which I shall presently bring under your notice.

(40.) The compounds whose names are written up in the third column of the two following tables occur either as natural products of the animal body, or as constituent residues of such natural products. In the first and second columns are given the names of the simpler molecules, by the mutual combination of which, with elimination of water, the corresponding bodies named in the third column are produced. I think I may venture to say that in every instance the bodies in this column have been proved to consist of the residues which they are here represented to contain, although, as I have said, in those bodies which are composed of more than two ultimate residues, the order in which the residues are successively combined, or the relation in which any two of them stand to the remainder, may be to some extent a matter of assumption. The word 'acid' is omitted from the columns for the sake of space :—

Residues		Diamerones
Alcohol	Sulphuric	Isethionic
Wood-spirit	Ammonia	Methylamine
Carbonic	Ammonia	Urea
Glycolic	Ammonia	Glycocine
Leucic	Ammonia	Leucine
Palmitic	Cetal	Spermaceti
Palmitic	Melyssal	Myricin
Palmitic	Glycerin	Palmitin
Stearic	Glycerin	Stearin
Oleic	Glycerin	Olein

(41.) The first of these bodies, namely, isethionic acid, is a constituent of taurine, and is formed by the union of alcohol and sulphuric acid with elimination of water, or, in other words, it contains a residue of each of these two bodies. Next on the list is methylamine, a frequent product of the putrefactive decomposition of animal matter. It contains a residue of wood-spirit and a residue of ammonia.

Then we come to urea, which contains a residue of carbonic acid and a residue of ammonia. In my first lecture I spoke of urea as being the ammoniated form of carbonic acid—as bearing to carbonic acid the same relation that ammonia bears to water—whereas I now represent it as a compound of carbonic acid and ammonia with elimination of water; but a little consideration will show that the two modes of regarding this and similar bodies are substantially the same. The empirical formula for carbonic acid—by which I mean hydrated carbonic acid—is CH_2O_3, while that for urea is CH_4N_2O. But regarding the two bodies as derivatives of the double atoms of water and ammonia respectively, or as the hydrate and amide of carbonyl, these formulæ become $(CO)''H_2O_2$, corresponding to H_4O_2, and $(CO)''H_4N_2$ corresponding to H_6N_2 respectively. Accordingly, the representation of urea as a compound of carbonic acid and ammonia with elimination of water, or as a variety of carbonic acid in which certain elements of water are replaced by the corresponding elements of ammonia, is shown in these almost identical equations:—

Carbonic acid	2-Ammonia	2-Water	Urea
$C H_2O_3$	$+\ H_6N_2$	$-\ H_4O_2$	$=\ C H_4N_2O$
$(CO)H_4O_2$	$+\ (H_2)H_4N_2$	$=\ (H_2)H_4O_2$	$+\ (CO)H_4N_2$

Glycocine, or sugar of gelatin, the next compound on the list, contains, as I have already observed, a residue of ammonia and a residue of glycolic or oxiacetic acid. Leucine, a body upon which I shall offer some observations in a future lecture, is a homologue of glycocine, and contains a residue of ammonia and a residue of leucic acid. We now come to spermaceti, which contains a residue of palmitic acid, an important member of our primary series of fatty acids, united with the residue of a solid alcohol, the cetylic, which bears to palmitic acid precisely the same relation that common ethylic alcohol bears to acetic acid, so that spermaceti is a true homologue of acetic ether, as shown in these equations:—

Acetic		Ethylic		Water		Acetic ether
$C_2H_4O_2$	+	C_2H_6O	−	H_2O	=	$C_4H_8O_2$
Palmitic		Cetylic		Water		Spermaceti
$C_{16}H_{32}O_2$	+	$C_{16}H_{34}O$	−	H_2O	=	$C_{32}H_{64}O_2$

Next, we have **myricin**, which forms from 60 to 80 per cent. of ordinary beeswax, and is composed of a residue of palmitic acid united with a residue of another solid alcohol, the melyssic, having the formula $C_{30}H_{62}O$. Myricin is formed according to the same typical equation as spermaceti and acetic ether, namely, $A + B - H_2O = X$; but the constituent palmitic acid, instead of being combined with the alcohol of its own group, is combined with the alcohol containing a double number of carbon atoms.

The three following bodies are selected as examples of the true fats. The first of them, namely, **palmitin**, is an important constituent of palm oil or butter, and also exists in human and other soft fats to a considerable extent. They are all three produced in accordance with the same typical equation, $3A + B - 3H_2O = X$, as shown below:—

Fatty acid		Glycerin		Water		
$3C_{16}H_{32}O_2$	+	$C_3H_8O_3$	−	$3H_2O$	=	Palmitin
$3C_{18}H_{36}O_2$	+	$C_3H_8O_3$	−	$3H_2O$	=	Stearin
$3C_{18}H_{34}O_2$	+	$C_3H_8O_3$	−	$3H_2O$	=	Olein

You observe that stearic acid is a homologue of palmitic acid, to which it stands next but one on the series; but oleic acid, which differs in composition from stearic acid by a deficiency of two hydrogen atoms, belongs to another set of compounds altogether, namely, the secondary series of fatty acids. The simplest known acid of this series is the acrolic, which is a member of the propionic group, and, as you may perceive by referring to the previous table of propionic compounds, bears to propionic acid the same relation that oleic bears to stearic acid.

COMPLEX ANIMAL PRODUCTS. 43

(42.) All the bodies in the table we have just considered contain the residues of what may be regarded as primary, or aplone, molecules; but one or other of the residues contained in the several compounds included in the next table is itself a complex body built up by the union of two or more simple molecules.

Residues		Polymerones
Isethionic	Ammonia	Taurine
Glycolic	Methylamine	Sarcosine
Carbonic	Urea	Allophan
Oxalic	Urea	Paraban
Mesoxalic	Urea	Alloxan
Benzoic	Glycocine	Hippuric
Cholic	Glycocine	Bile acid α
Cholic	Taurine	Bile acid β
Urea	Sarcosine	Kreatine
Urea	Methylamine	Methyluramine

Thus taurine, of which I am able, through the kindness of Mr. Lloyd Bullock, to exhibit an extremely handsome specimen, contains a residue of ammonia united with a residue of isethionic acid, which already contains a residue of alcohol and a residue of sulphuric acid. Sarcosine, which is a constituent of kreatine, contains a residue of glycolic acid and a residue of methylamine, which itself contains a residue of wood-spirit and a residue of ammonia. Allophan is a purely artificial compound, closely related to paraban and alloxan, which are products of the oxidation of uric acid. These three bodies contain respectively a residue of carbonic acid CH_2O_3, of oxalic acid $C_2H_2O_4$, and of mesoxalic acid $C_3H_2O_5$, combined with a residue of urea, which itself contains a residue of carbonic acid and a residue of ammonia. The constitution of all three bodies is expressed by the same typical equation $A + B - 2H_2O = X$, as exemplified below in the case of alloxan:—

Urea		Mesoxalic		Water		Alloxan
CH_4N_2O	+	$C_3H_2O_5$	−	$2H_2O$	=	$C_4H_2N_2O_4$

We next come to **hippuric acid**, which, as I have already said, contains a residue of benzoic acid and a residue of glycocine, which itself contains residues of glycolic acid and ammonia. This is succeeded by the two principal acids of the bile, the first of which, or **glyco-cholic acid**, contains a residue of cholic acid and a residue of glycocine, and consequently differs only from hippuric acid in containing a residue of cholic acid $C_{24}H_{40}O_5$, instead of a residue of benzoic acid $C_7H_6O_2$. The other bile acid, known as **tauro-cholic acid**, contains a residue of cholic acid and a residue of taurine, which already contains residues of ammonia and isethionic acid, the latter body further containing a residue of alcohol and a residue of sulphuric acid, thus:—

$$\text{Tauro-cholic} \begin{cases} \text{Cholic} \\ \text{Taurine} \begin{cases} \text{Ammonia} \\ \text{Isethionic} \begin{cases} \text{Alcohol} \\ \text{Sulphuric} \end{cases} \end{cases} \end{cases}$$

(43.) The last compound which I propose to bring under your notice to-day is **kreatine**, a beautiful crystalline body, as you may perceive, from the unusually fine specimen lent me by Dr. Hugo Müller. This body, which exists largely in the juice of flesh, and also, though to much less amount, in human urine, is represented by the formula $C_4H_9N_3O_2$. Under the influence of caustic baryta it absorbs water, with transformation into sarcosine and urea, the residues of which pre-exist in the kreatine, thus:—

Urea		Sarcosine		Water		Kreatine
CH_4N_2O	+	$C_3H_7NO_2$	−	H_2O	=	$C_4H_9N_3O_2$

The urea, as I have already observed, contains residues of carbonic acid and ammonia, and the sarcosine residues of glycolic acid and methylamine, which last body further contains a residue of ammonia and a residue of wood-spirit, as shown in this diagram:—

CONSTITUTION OF KREATINE.

Kreatine
{
  Urea { Carbonic / Ammonia
  Sarcosine { Glycolic / Methylamine { Wood-spirit / Ammonia
}

We have seen that the glycolic residue of hippuric acid may be got rid of by oxidation, so as to leave the benzoic and ammonia residues combined with one another in the form of benzamide. Similarly the glycolic residue of kreatine may be got rid of by oxidation, so as to leave the urea and methylamine residues combined with one another in the form of **methyluramine** or methyl-guanidine, thus:—

Urea	Methylamine	Water	Methyluramine
CH_4N_2O +	CH_5N −	H_2O =	$C_2H_7N_3$

Concluding with these extremely complex animal products, I trust I have satisfied you of the main position with which we started, that highly complex molecules are built up of the residues of comparatively simple molecules, which are capable for the most part of being referred to definite positions in certain natural series or groups of associated bodies—in such series as those of the aromatic and fatty acids, aldehydes, alcohols, &c., and in such groups as the benzoic, acetic, propionic, and butyric groups for instance.

LECTURE III.

Recapitulation—Statical and dynamical aspects of organic chemistry—Destruction and construction of constituent molecules—Tendency of oxidation to produce molecules with fewer and fewer carbon and hydrogen atoms—Final production of carb-anhydride CO_2, and water H_2O—Destructive or analytic phase of organic chemistry—Natural synthesis of organic compounds attended by deoxidation—Liberation of oxygen by growing vegetables—Tendency of deoxidation to combine separate carbon and hydrogen atoms into complex molecules—Vegetable tissue and secretion formed by deoxidation of carbonic anhydride and water—Imperfect knowledge of intermediate products—Formation of nitrogenised tissues—Ammonia in its relation to plant life—Correlations of ammonia, nitrous acid, and nitrogen—Deoxidation of nitrous acid by plants—Manurial equivalency of nitrous acid and ammonia—Existence of nitrogen in natural organic products as a residue of ammonia—Artificial synthesis of organic bodies—Combination of constituent molecules with one another—Elementary formation of constituent molecules—Historical remarks on organic synthesis—Alleged incompetency of chemical, and necessity for vital action—Artificial production of all organic compounds by purely chemical means—Kolbe's indirect formation of acetic acid from carbon, hydrogen, and oxygen, in 1845—Subsequent advances by Berthelot and others—Oxidation of hydrogen into water, and of carbon into carbonic anhydride—Evolution of light and heat—Deoxidation of water and carbonic anhydride into hydrogen and carbon—Similar separations of oxygen from hydrogen and carbon effected by living plant and by artificial processes—Comparison of deoxidising vegetal and oxidising animal functions—Nature of forces concerned in respective actions.

(44.) I STATED in my last lecture that chemists were acquainted with a great number of monobasic organic acids, containing two atoms of oxygen in their respective molecules, and that these acids were capable of being arranged in two principal classes, known as the aromatic class and the fatty class, and exemplified in the accompanying lists :—

Fatty Acids		Aromatic Acids	
Formic	$C H_2 O_2$	Collic ?	$C_6 H_4 O_2$
Acetic	$C_2 H_4 O_2$	Benzoic	$C_7 H_6 O_2$
Propionic	$C_3 H_6 O_2$	Toluic	$C_8 H_8 O_2$
Butyric	$C_4 H_8 O_2$	Picic	$C_9 H_{10} O_2$
Valeric	$C_5 H_{10} O_2$	Cuminic	$C_{10} H_{12} O_2$
,,		,,	
Melissic	$C_{30} H_{60} O_2$		

The acids of these two series presented, I told you, a marked parallelism in their constitution, seriation, and properties; and, moreover, when submitted to the action of the same chemical reagents, underwent precisely analogous metamorphoses. I dwelt still more upon the mutual resemblance manifested by consecutive members of the same series, and pointed out that even the most remote members were distinguished from one another by gradational differences only. I observed, also, that each one of these primary monobasic acids, fatty or aromatic, was associated with a more or less complete set of congeners, which differed from it in constitution and properties, but were correlated with it by the circumstance of their containing the same number of carbon atoms, and still more markedly by their derivation from, and convertibility into it and one another—that acetic acid $C_2H_4O_2$, for instance, was associated with the less oxidised bodies, olefiant gas C_2H_4, alcohol C_2H_6O, and aldehyd C_2H_4O, as well as with the more highly oxidised glycolic and oxalic acids, $C_2H_4O_3$ and $C_2H_2O_4$, respectively—to such an extent, indeed, that they might all be regarded as varieties of one and the same primitive molecule. I further went on to say that the complex tissue products of the animal and vegetable kingdoms were built up of the residues of these fatty and aromatic acids, and of their respective congeners; so that, upon breaking up such tissue products into their constituent molecules, we were, in the great majority of instances, able, even at the present time, to refer the constituent molecules to their appropriate positions in certain definite series and groups; and had every reason to believe that with increasing knowledge we should be able to make the assignment in every instance.

(45.) Moreover, in my first lecture I pointed out to you that organic chemistry had a statical aspect which related to the composition of bodies, and a dynamical aspect which related to their changes of composition. But in all that I have hitherto observed I have had regard principally to the statical aspect of the question. I have glanced, indeed, at the mutual metamorphosis by oxidation and deoxidation of compounds belonging to the same natural group; and have referred more fully to the combination of their several residues with one another in forming complex tissue products, and to the separation of the completed residues from one another in the breaking up of these products; but I have not yet considered the mode in which the primary constituent molecules are themselves produced, or yet the mode in which, when once produced, it is possible for us to destroy them, and to these points I will now direct your attention.

(46.) If we treat the more complex members of our series of fatty acids, for instance, with powerful oxidising agents, we obtain bodies in which the number of the constituent atoms of hydrogen and carbon becomes progressively less and less, until we arrive at bodies containing only two, and finally at bodies containing only one carbon-atom. In some cases these successive oxidation products are found to contain the same number of atoms of oxygen as the bodies from which they were produced, though in the majority of instances they contain a greater number, and consequently belong to more oxygenised series. But whether they contain the same or a greater number of oxygen atoms, we find the number of their atoms of carbon and hydrogen become gradually less and less, their molecules pertaining to simpler and simpler groupings. For example, the following intermediate compounds, among many others, have been successively obtained by oxidising stearic acid $C_{18}H_{36}O_2$, with nitric acid of moderate strength:—

	Oxidation Products	
Rutic acid	$C_{10}H_{20}O_2$	
Suberic		$C_8H_{14}O_4$
Œnanthic	$C_7H_{14}O_2$	
Pimelic		$C_7H_{12}O_4$
Caproic	$C_6H_{12}O_2$	
Adipic		$C_6H_{10}O_4$
Butyric	$C_4H_8O_2$	
Succinic		$C_4H_6O_4$

(47.) The tendency of oxidation, then, is to separate the constituent carbon and hydrogen atoms from one another, until at last there is left only the most stable mono-carbon compound known to chemists, namely, carbonic anhydride, or, as it is frequently called, carbonic acid. No matter what the complexity of the original molecule, the chemist eventually succeeds in transforming it by oxidation, though a series of less and less complex molecules, into carb-anhydride, or oxide of carbon, on the one hand, and water, or oxide of hydrogen, on the other—the identical bodies out of which the vegetable organism directly, and the animal organism indirectly, builds up those complex bodies which we have designated proximate organic principles. As was observed by Gerhardt some twenty years ago, 'one of the two extremities of the scale of organic compounds is occupied by albumin, and gelatin, and fat, and cerebral matter; the other extremity by carbonic acid, and water, and ammonia; while an infinity of bodies are included in the interval. The chemist, by treating the superior substances with oxidising agents, gradually descends the scale of complexity, converting these substances into more and more simple products, by successively burning off a portion of their carbon and hydrogen.'

(48.) Thus, then, we have presented to us one important aspect of organic chemistry, namely, its analytic or destructive aspect; that aspect upon which, until of late years, the attention of chemists was almost exclusively directed; that aspect, indeed, which was at one time considered to be the only possible aspect that could ever be presented. To quote again from the same distinguished chemist, of whom I am always proud to avow myself a pupil: 'I show,' said Gerhardt, writing in 1842, 'how the chemist does everything that is contrary to living nature—that he burns, destroys, works by analysis—the vital force alone operates by synthesis and reconstructs the edifice destroyed by chemical forces.' But, in reality, there is another side to the shield; there is a constructive as well as a destructive, a synthetic as well as an analytic organic chemistry; and to this view of the subject I will now direct your attention.

(49.) I need scarcely remind you of the mode in which vegetable structures are built up. The minute seed grows into the gigantic tree, the great mass of which is made up of carbon, hydrogen, and oxygen, that the living organism has stored up from the carbonic acid and water with which it has been supplied throughout the period of its existence, and which it has inter-combined into the various forms of vegetable tissue. Now, this storing up of carbon, hydrogen, and oxygen—this formation of vegetable compounds—is attended throughout by an evolution of oxygen. The proportion of oxygen contained in carbonic acid and water being greatly in excess of the proportion contained in vegetable tissue and secretion, we have throughout the growth of every plant a constant deoxidation of carbonic acid and water—the carbon, hydrogen, and necessary oxygen being retained in the substance of the plant, the oxygen in excess of the requirements of the plant being discharged into the atmosphere. Let me recall to your recollection one of the original experiments of Priestley upon this subject. He showed, for example, that under exposure to sunlight, a quickly-growing leafy plant, immersed in an atmosphere which by the combustion of fuel had been freed from oxygen and charged with carbonic acid, gradually restored that atmosphere to its pristine condition, by an absorption and subsequent decomposition of its carbonic acid into oxygen gas evolved from the leaves, and carbon retained within the vegetable structure. Here we have an imitation of the experiment. A bunch of fresh mint has been thrust into this narrow cylinder of dilute carbonic acid water standing in the small pneumatic trough, and the whole exposed to sunlight. You perceive that the leaves are now covered all over with minute beads of gas, and that a small but appreciable quantity of gas has collected at the top of the cylinder. By pulling the attached thread I am able to withdraw the bunch of mint, and on now passing up a few bubbles of nitric oxide, a dark-brown vapour is produced at the top of the cylinder, proving the contained gas to be oxygen; which oxygen, gradually evolved by the growing plant, has been separated by the plant from the carbonic acid, or hydrated oxide of carbon, wherewith it was surrounded.

(50.) Now, just as oxidation tends to break up the constituent carbon and hydrogen atoms of a complex organic molecule into simpler and simpler bodies, so, on the other hand, do we find that deoxidation tends to combine the separated carbon and hydrogen atoms into more and more complex bodies. The organism of a plant, for instance, operating upon monocarbon molecules only, effects simultaneously their deoxidation and inter-combination. It deoxidates them with evolution of oxygen into the atmosphere, and combines the residual less oxygenated carbon and hydrogen into the various forms of vegetable tissue and secretion. What the intermediate stages are between water and carbonic acid, on the one hand, and some vegetable principle such as mannite or sugar on the other, we cannot positively say, though our knowledge upon the subject is receiving daily accessions. But be our acquaintance with the intermediate stages ever so imperfect, the final result is perfectly intelligible. We know, for instance, that in the production of this body, mannite, there has been a deoxidation of six molecules of carbonic anhydride and seven molecules of water, and that in the course of the deoxidation, the thirteen separate molecules have been conjoined into one single molecule, thus:—

Carb-anhydride	Water	Oxygen	Mannite
$6\ CO_2$ +	$7\ H_2O$ −	$13\ O$ =	$1\ C_6H_{14}O_6$

(51.) This, then, is the point which I wish to bring prominently under your notice—that while oxidation tends to the separation of atoms, and the formation of simple out of complex bodies, deoxidation, as manifested in the vegetable kingdom, tends to the combination of atoms, or to the formation of complex bodies out of simple ones. Now, the chemist in his laboratory can imitate, however crudely, this synthesis of nature. We find in the laboratory, as in the organism, that deoxidation, actual or potential, leads to the conjunction of atoms, and to the building up of complex molecules. In broad antagonism to the doctrines which only a few years back were regarded as indisputable, we now find that the chemist, like the plant, is capable of producing from carbonic acid and water a whole host of organic bodies, and we see no reason to question his ultimate ability to reproduce all animal and vegetable principles whatsoever.

(52.) But for the production of certain organic principles, whether by natural or artificial means, something more than carbonic acid and water is required. The albuminoid bodies, in particular, cannot be formed without nitrogen, and plants, in general, cannot grow without a supply of ammonia or some transformable compound. You will observe, however, that ammonia, considered as a pabulum for plants, differs in this important respect from both carbonic anhydride and water, that it is not susceptible of deoxidation, or amenable, in other words, to the characteristic chemical action of plant-life. On the contrary, ammonia is the most thoroughly deoxidised, or rather hydrogenetted, compound of nitrogen with which chemists are acquainted. Even nitrogen itself may be looked upon as less deoxidised than ammonia, being intermediate between ammonia and nitrous acid, thus:—

Nitrogen Molecules

$H N O_3$	Nitric acid
$H N O_2$	Nitrous acid
$N N$	Nitrogen
$H_3 N$	Ammonia

The nitric and nitrous acids being regarded as oxidised forms of nitrogen, ammonia must be regarded as a deoxidised form, the element *quoad* its state of oxidation being strictly intermediate between ammonia and nitrous acid, as I hope to render experimentally evident to you.

(53.) Thus, on passing a series of electric sparks from the Rühmkorff machine through the moist air contained in this apparently empty glass cylinder, a portion of the nitrogen of the contained air becomes gradually oxidised, and after a short time we shall see brown nitrous fumes make their appearance, in accordance with this reaction:—

Nitrogen		Oxygen		Water		Nitrous acid
N_2	+	O_3	+	H_2O	=	$2\,HNO_2$

By allowing the experiment to continue, the depth of colour in the cylinder will go on increasing so as to be visible from every part of the theatre. But I dare say I shall be able to render the nitrous acid already produced abundantly manifest, by allowing it to act upon a piece of paper stencilled with starch and iodide of potassium solution. That we have really obtained a considerable amount of nitrous acid, by the few sparks which have as yet passed through the air in the cylinder, is shown by the speedy liberation of iodine from the iodide of potassium, and consequent appearance of the word NITROUS in purple characters upon the prepared paper.

(54.) Now for the reverse experiment. In this flask is a mixture of materials for generating hydrogen, namely, a little granulated zinc, some iron borings, and warm solution of potash. Active effervescence quickly takes place, and the evolved gas, which is without action on turmeric paper, as you perceive, burns with the characteristic flame of hydrogen. If we now absorb the brown nitrous fumes contained in this gas-bottle, by agitation with aqueous potash, and pour the solution so produced of nitrite and nitrate of potassium into our hydrogen flask, you observe that the effervescence becomes more rapid, and that the evolved gas is now decidedly ammoniacal, as shown by its browning the turmeric paper and fuming with the hydrochloric acid vapour I bring into its neighbourhood. The reaction taking place in the flask is represented in this equation,—

Nitrous acid		Hydrogen		Water		Ammonia
HNO_3	$+$	H_6	$=$	$2H_2O$	$+$	H_3N ;

so that not only is oxygen taken away from, but hydrogen is added to the nitrogen of our original nitrous acid.

(55.) By combining the oxidised form of nitrogen, or nitrous acid HNO_2, with the hydrogenetted form of nitrogen, or ammonia H_3N, we obtain nitrite of ammonia NH_3HNO_2, a neutral crystallisable salt, whose somewhat concentrated solution is contained in this flask-retort. Now, on applying heat to the retort, observe what takes place. There is, you see, a copious evolution of gas, some of which we will collect over the pneumatic trough; and, in order to save time, will content ourselves with only a small cylinder full. The gas, produced in this manner from the nitrite of ammonia solution in the retort, is nitrogen, recognisable at once by its property of extinguishing flame. In this decomposition then the hydrogen of the ammonia exactly suffices to remove the excess of oxygen from the nitrous acid, whereby the nitrogen of both constituents of the salt is simultaneously liberated, thus :—

Ammonia nitrite		Water		Nitrogen
NH_3HNO_2	$=$	$2H_2O$	$+$	N_2

Hence nitrogen may be looked upon as exactly intermediate in its state of oxidation between nitrous acid on the one hand, and ammonia on the other; whilst ammonia must be considered the extreme product of deoxidation. Accordingly, it has been found as a general result both of laboratory and field experiments, the latter conducted more especially by Messrs. Lawes and Gilbert in this country, that cereals and other plants thrive equally well upon salts of nitrous or nitric acid as upon salts of ammonia; and that when a plant is supplied with water, carbonic acid, and nitrous acid, it exerts upon the nitrous acid the same sort of reducing action that it does upon the water and carbonic acid, whereby not only amylaceous, but ammoniated or nitrogenised principles are abundantly produced. Indeed some chemists have maintained that nitrous acid, rather than ammonia, forms the normal nitrogenous food of plants, and that the ammonia of cultivated soil is habitually converted into nitrous acid before its absorption by their rootlets.

(56.) Be this as it may, in all animal and vegetable nitrogenised products of which the constitution is understood we know, and in all other such principles have good reason to believe, that the constituent nitrogen exists as a group apart—as a residue of, or proxy for, ammonia—ready on the occurrence of suitable conditions to regenerate that ammonia. As was observed by Laurent some ten years ago, 'nitrogen does not enter into the constitution of organic substances on the same footing, so to speak, as do the other bodies. Organic compounds seem to consist of carbon, hydrogen, and oxygen only; whilst nitrogen exists therein but as the representative of ammonia on the one hand, or of nitric acid on the other.' In organic compounds of natural origin, nitrogen occurs only as a residue of ammonia; whilst in organic compounds of artificial origin, it occurs sometimes as a residue of ammonia, as in cyanogen C_2N_2, sometimes as a residue of nitric acid, as in azobenzide $C_{12}H_{10}N_2$.

(57.) In the artificial formation of organic compounds, then, there are two distinct points for our consideration, namely, the building up of the primary oxihydrocarbon molecules, and the combination of the residues of these molecules with one another, and with ammonia, to form complex organic principles. Now, the power of combining the residues of aplone molecules with one another, so as to form more or less complex bodies, has been in the possession of chemists from almost the earliest days of organic chemistry, and has been fully recognised to be in their possession. But, somewhat strangely, it is only of late years that this well-known power has been applied to the construction of some of the most familiar components of animal and vegetable bodies. It is only of late years, for instance, that chemists have produced stearin, by putting together the residues of glycerin and the fatty acid; or sarcosine, by putting together the residues of acetic acid and methylamine; or hippuric acid, by putting together the residues of benzoic acid and glycocine; or taurine, by putting together the residues of isethionic acid and ammonia, &c., as referred to in my last lecture. It must be observed, however, that the neglect of these syntheses did not arise so much from want of interest in the production of the bodies, as from want of knowledge of their intimate constitution. No sooner, for instance, was the constitution of the above four compounds satisfactorily made out than they were obtained artificially by Berthelot, Volhard, Dessaignes, and Strecker and Kolbe respectively; and as it has been with these, so doubtless will it be with many other complex tissue products, with the constitution of which we are as yet imperfectly acquainted.

(58.) The first stage of the process of organic synthesis, however, or the building up of the primary oxihydrocarbon molecules, was considered until very recently as altogether beyond the art of the chemist. It used to be thought that chemistry was essentially incompetent to the production not only of organised, but of organic bodies. For the production of these bodies, the intervention of some living organism, the expenditure of some vital force—whatever that might be—was considered absolutely necessary. While the constituent atoms of a piece of alum, for instance, were admittedly held together by mere mechanical and chemical forces, the atoms of a piece of sugar, on the other hand, or of a piece of fat, were conceived to be put together in some mysterious way by vital forces. These opinions were originally propounded by Berzelius at a time when the then state of knowledge may possibly have justified their enunciation. They remained almost unchallenged for a long series of years, and are still asserted in some recent text-books with a degree of dogmatism altogether opposed to the present advanced state of knowledge on the subject.

(59.) The great progress recently made in the constructive art of the chemist is, I think, a topic of sufficient interest to warrant me in entering into further detail upon the heretofore accepted opinions, which I find expressed very well in the last edition but one of Liebig's Chemical Letters—the last edition that was translated by Dr. Gregory, who, writing in 1851, says:—

'We are able to construct a crystal of alum from its elements, namely, sulphur, oxygen, hydrogen, potassium, and aluminum, inasmuch as heat as well as chemical affinity are, within a certain limit, at our free disposal, and thus we can determine the manner of arrangement of the simple and compound elements. But we cannot make an atom of sugar from the elements of sugar, because in their aggregation into the characteristic form of a sugar atom, the vital force co-operates, which is not within the reach of our control, as heat, light, the force of gravity, &c., are to a certain extent. . . . . We may produce atoms of a higher order by combining two, three, four, or more compound organic atoms; we can decompose the more complex into less complex compound atoms; we can produce sugar from wood or starch, and from sugar we can produce oxalic acid, lactic acid, butyric acid, acetic acid, aldehyd, alcohol, formic acid, &c., although we are altogether incapable of producing any of these compounds by a direct combination of their elements.'

(60.) I might further refer you to Dr. Gregory's deservedly-popular Handbook, of which the last edition appeared in 1857, and to many other works, as showing the general prevalence of these opinions, but content myself with extracting the following series of passages from the most recent of all our chemical manuals. You will see that in this work, published only two years ago, the statements made by Liebig in 1851, and by older chemists long before then, are substantially reiterated. 'Organic chemistry,' say the authors, 'is that branch of the science which refers to the properties and composition of organised products, or of substances which have been formed in vegetables and animals under the influence of *life*. . . . The *products*, or those substances which result from artificial processes, are far more numerous than the *educts*, or proximate principles of which organic compounds are considered to be formed. These educts, which, as their name implies, may be extracted in an unaltered state, are the immediate or *proximate* principles of the vegetable or animal structure. . . . Some bodies which exist naturally in the vegetable structure, and are regarded as educts, may be artificially produced by a reaction of mineral on organic substances. In all cases, however, either an organic substance or a body derived from the organic kingdom is indispensable to this conversion. . . . The principal sources of hydrocyanic acid are certain metallic cyanides. But these compounds have an organic origin; they are the products of a reaction of organic upon inorganic substances; hence the production of hydrocyanic acid by their decomposition furnishes no exception to the remark above made. Under this point of view, the production of artificial urea from hydrated cyanate of ammonia is simply a conversion of cyanic acid (a derivative of an organic substance) into another organic compound. By no processes yet known can gum, starch, or sugar be produced from their elementary constituents C, H, O; and by the production of alcohol from a mixture of sulphuric acid, olefiant gas, and water, Berthelot has merely proved that a hydrocarbon of organic origin or one derived from organic matter is capable of being converted into another organic product.' Thus the view very generally entertained but a few years back was substantially this—that the chemist could not produce organic out of mineral matter; he might transform one kind of organic matter into some allied kind of organic matter— starch into sugar, and olefiant gas into alcohol, for instance; he might produce certain simple organic principles by the breaking up of more complex molecules—oil of spiræa, for instance, from salicin, alcohol from sugar, and glycerin from fat; and he might even produce highly complex principles, by a conjunction of two or more simple principles—oil of wintergreen by combining salicic acid with wood spirit, and fat by combining stearic acid, for instance, with glycerin; but this was the limit of his powers—he might shuffle about the residues of existing organic compounds in a variety of ways, but was utterly unable to produce even the simplest of them by elemental synthesis.

(61.) Our present knowledge, however, assures that these opinions are altogether without foundation. Already hundreds of organic principles have been built up from their constituent elements, and as I have previously said, there is now no reason to doubt our capability of producing all organic principles whatsoever in a similar manner. Wöhler's artificial production of urea from cyanate of ammonia in 1828, and Pelouze's artificial production of formic from hydrocyanic acid in 1831, were in reality very important pioneering achievements, although cyanogen and its compounds were at that time known only as products of the decomposition of organic bodies. But in 1845, Kolbe produced acetic acid from carbon by a series of strictly inorganic reactions, and thereby laid the foundation of modern synthetic chemistry. The successive steps of his process are shown in the following table:—

Acetic Acid Synthesis

CS_2	Carbon disulphide
CCl_4	Carbon tetrachloride
C_2Cl_4	Tetrachlor-ethylene
$C_2HCl_3O_2$	Trichlor-acetic acid
$C_2H_4O_2$	Acetic acid

Disulphide of carbon CS_2, was first obtained by the combustion of charcoal in sulphur vapour. This compound was next acted upon by chlorine at a high temperature, whereby it was converted into chloride of sulphur and chloride of carbon CCl_4. Then by transmission through red-hot tubes, this last product was transformed, with evolution of chlorine, into the so-called sesquichloride of carbon, $2CCl_4 = Cl_2 + C_2Cl_6$, and eventually into the so-called bichloride of carbon or tetrachlor-ethylene, $C_2Cl_6 = Cl_2 + C_2Cl_4$. In the course of his examination of this tetrachlor-ethylene, Kolbe observed that by exposure to chlorine in presence of water, it was decomposed into a mixture of hydrochloric and trichlor-acetic acids, thus:—

Chlor-ethylene	Water	Chlorine		Chlorhydric		Chlor-acetic
C_2Cl_4 +	$2H_2O$ +	Cl_2	=	$3HCl$	+	$C_2HCl_3O_2$

Then by subjecting this trichlor-acetic acid to the action of nascent hydrogen, he successively converted it into dichlor-acetic acid $C_2H_2Cl_2O_2$, monochlor-acetic acid $C_2H_3ClO_2$, and finally into normal acetic acid $C_2H_4O_2$. In concluding his account of these singular transformations, Kolbe remarked with great prescience: —' From the foregoing observations we deduce the interesting fact that acetic acid, hitherto known only as a product of the oxidation of organic materials, can be built up by almost direct synthesis from its elements. . . . If we could but transform acetic acid into alcohol, and out of the latter could obtain sugar and starch, we should then be enabled to build up these common vegetable principles, by the so-called artificial method, from their most ultimate elements.'

(62.) Relying upon these results, Laurent in his ' Méthode de Chimie,' 1853, and Hofmann in a course of lectures ' On Organic Chemistry,' delivered the same year at the Royal Institution, the latter, with very great detail, showed how impossible it was to draw the line of demarcation between carbon compounds of organic, and carbon compounds of mineral origin. They both referred to Kolbe's formation from mineral elements of acetic acid or vinegar, and of certain highly complex bodies procurable from vinegar, such as mesidine $C_9H_{13}N$, and nitro-mesidine $C_9H_{12}N_2O_2$. It must be admitted, however, that to the labours of Berthelot, prosecuted unintermittingly for the last ten years, is due that full recognition of synthetic organic chemistry which now obtains, and the very great advances recently made therein both by himself and by others, which I purpose hereafter to bring under your more especial consideration.

Before proceeding, however, to exemplify the powers of organic synthesis in the artificial formation of animal and vegetable products from carbon, hydrogen, and oxygen, I must beg leave to make a rather long digression. I propose, firstly, to bring before you some elementary experiments connected with the production and decomposition of the oxides of carbon and hydrogen, or carbonic anhydride CO_2, and water H_2O, respectively; and then to consider with you what bearing these experiments have upon the forces exerted in animal and vegetable life, or, in other words, upon the so-called vital forces.

(63.) I have here an ordinary form of apparatus in which hydrogen gas is being generated in the usual manner from zinc and dilute sulphuric acid, and dried by transmission through oil of vitriol. On burning the jet of dried hydrogen under this cold bell jar, we observe that the interior of the jar becomes quickly covered with a film of condensed steam or water, produced by the direct combination of the hydrogen gas with the oxygen of the air; and, by properly contrived experiments, I might show that the weight of water produced in this way is exactly equal to the weight of oxygen and hydrogen consumed in the burning. But during the combustion of the gases there is a production not only of water, but of heat; which I may exhibit to you in a more striking manner. We have here a piece of clean platinum foil, which is now maintained in a state of ignition by the hydrogen flame. I turn off the supply of hydrogen for a minute or so, and before the platinum has become quite cold, turn it on again, when you observe that the metal becomes and continues feebly red-hot without inflaming the gas. The mixed hydrogen and air on the surface of the foil combine with one another to form water, and at the same time produce an amount of heat sufficient to maintain the metal in a state of visible ignition. But where does this heat come from? We have a production of heat and a production of water; ought we not to account for the one as intelligibly as we do for the other?

(64.) I now take a piece of charcoal, and make it red-hot in the Bunsen gas flame. Having first poured a little lime-water into the bottle of oxygen, to show the result of the action, I next introduce the glowing charcoal, when combination between the gas and charcoal takes place, you perceive, with vivid combustion. In this experiment, then, we have carbonic anhydride or di-oxide of carbon formed, the source of which is perfectly evident; and upon shaking up the resulting gas with the clear lime-water we previously poured into the bottle, that which was soluble hydrate of calcium becomes insoluble carbonate of calcium or chalk, whereby we have as you see, a considerable white turbidity produced, thus:—

Carb-anhyd.	Lime		Water	Chalk
CO_2 +	$\{ H_2Ca''O_2$ or	=	H_2O +	$\{ CCa''O_3$ or
	$CaO.H_2O$			$CaO.CO_2$

If instead of absorbing it by lime-water in this manner, we were directly or indirectly to weigh the resulting carb-anhydride, we should find that its weight was exactly equal to that of the carbon burnt, plus that of the oxygen which served to burn it. But, in addition to carbonic anhydride, there was during the combination an abundant production of light and heat. Now the axiom, that out of nothing comes nothing, is just as true of light and heat as of water and carbonic anhydride. We have no difficulty in understanding the production of the carbonic anhydride; what, however, is the origin of the light and heat?

(65.) So much, then, for the formation of oxide of hydrogen or water, and oxide of carbon or carbonic anhydride; now for their decompositions. By a variety of means we are able to separate hydrogen and carbon from their respective combinations with oxygen—one of the most suitable materials for the purpose being metallic sodium. If, for instance, we introduce under this inverted jar of water a piece of metallic sodium, which, for the sake of convenience, I have diluted with a little mercury, so that the reaction may take place more slowly than it otherwise would, we get, you perceive, a regular evolution of hydrogen gas. The sodium combines with the oxygen of the water, whilst its hydrogen is set at liberty; and in a similar manner we may liberate carbon from carbonic anhydride, as I will now endeavour to show you. The carbonic anhydride that we produced by the combustion of a piece of charcoal in oxygen was absorbed, you will remember, by means of lime, whereby we obtained this precipitate of chalk, from which by treatment with hydrochloric acid we may easily re-obtain the carbonic anhydride. Thus, if I transfer our mixture of chalk and water into the narrow cylinder standing over this mercurial trough, and then pass up a little hydrochloric acid, you see that the chalk disappears with effervescence, while a quantity of gas collects at the top of the cylinder, which is the carbonic anhydride we lately produced in this large gas-bottle by the direct combination of charcoal and oxygen:—

Chalk		Chlorhydric		Chlor-calcium		Water		Carb-anhyd.
$CaO.CO_2$	+	$2HCl$	=	$CaCl_2$	+	H_2O	+	CO_2

In the arrangement on the table before you, we are producing a current of carbonic anhydride in a similar manner, by acting upon chalk or, rather, marble, with dilute hydrochloric acid. The gas evolved in the Woulfe's bottle is transmitted over pumice and oil of vitriol to render it dry, and then conveyed to the bottom of an ordinary Florence flask, into which I have dropped a piece of clean metallic sodium. We now apply a large blowpipe flame to the bottom of the flask so as to heat the contained sodium. There is a little practical difficulty in starting the reaction, and perhaps the experiment may not succeed at the first trial, but it is sure to succeed sooner or later. The action is now beginning, and you observe the piece of sodium glowing in the flask. The glowing is soon succeeded by a brilliant combustion, attended by the formation of copious white fumes. The sodium has effected a decomposition of some of the carbonic anhydride, united with its oxygen to form soda, and liberated its carbon in the form of a black mass, which remains, as you see, at the bottom of the flask.

(66.) The piece of charcoal in this flask then has been extracted from carbonic anhydride, which is itself producible, as I have shown you, by the direct combustion of charcoal in air or oxygen. So that when we act upon oxide of hydrogen with sodium, we separate the oxygen and obtain the hydrogen; and when we act upon oxide of carbon with sodium we separate the oxygen and obtain the carbon. Now the living plant effects a similar decomposition of these two compounds, but in a gradual manner, which we shall hereafter endeavour to imitate. The plant absorbs oxide of hydrogen or water, and oxide of carbon or carbonic anhydride; deoxidises both compounds to a more or less complete extent; evolves the separated oxygen into the atmosphere; and retains the united carbon and hydrogen, with or without some oxygen, in the form of vegetable tissue or secretion. When the tissue or secretion is subjected to a full red heat, it yields, among other products, free carbon, free hydrogen, and various compounds of carbon with hydrogen. The piece of wood-charcoal now in my hand, for instance, has resulted indirectly from a gradual deoxidation of carbonic anhydride by the living plant, just as this other piece of charcoal in the flask has resulted directly from a violent deoxidation of carbonic anhydride by the metallic sodium.

(67.) Thus, then, we have presented to our notice the most important terrene, or rather cosmical function of plant life. The living plant effects a decomposition of carbonic anhydride and water, evolves the liberated oxygen, and retains within its organism the united carbon and hydrogen, which becoming the food of animals, are simultaneously disunited and re-oxidised once more into carbonic anhydride and water. Now, I wish to consider with you—I was going to say more minutely, but I should rather say more broadly—what is the essence of these complementary actions in their relation to the first principles of that dynamical philosophy which is often spoken of as the science of energetics. It formed part of my original plan to give merely a passing glance at this subject, and I certainly should not have ventured to discuss it in the elementary form in which I now propose to bring it under your notice, had it not recently come to my knowledge that certain principles of mechanical philosophy admitted by that class of naturalists who are called physicists, to be as fundamental even as the laws of gravitation, are not generally acknowledged by that other class of naturalists who are called physicians. Now, in order to contrast with one another the great antagonistic function of plants and animals—the decomposition of carbonic anhydride and water by the one class, and recomposition of carbonic anhydride and water by the other—it would not conduce to my object, even if it were within my competency, to discuss with you the simplest functions of organic life, as manifested by the most minute and simple organisms, in some of which it is scarcely possible for us to distinguish between the animal or vegetable character. Feeling that every phase of life deserves our attentive examination, I am far from insensible to the advantages attending the study of its most elementary forms. But this study cannot, I maintain, teach us the whole truth. There are principles of the highest importance which can only be learned by having regard to the directions in which animal and vegetable life respectively tend—by comparing with another the highly differentiated forms of animal and vegetable life, not in their minute details, but in their broad general features. In my next lecture, then, we shall have to consider more especially what is the nature of the force exerted in the characteristic actions of vegetable and animal life—whether we have to do with some peculiar internal vital force, or only with the ordinary external forces of nature, working in a manner strictly parallel to that in which they are habitually exerted in the inorganic world.

LECTURE IV.

External relations of vegetable and animal processes—Nature of cosmical forces—Mutual convertibility of heat and motion—Their quantitative equivalency with one another—Illustrations of motion resulting from muscular effort—Force rendered latent in mechanical separation of attracting bodies—Actual and potential energy—Chemical separation of attracting bodies—Theory of electrolysis—Force of galvanic battery derived from combustion of zinc—Heat of dissolving zinc manifested externally in ignition of platinum wire—The same heat stored up in electrolytic oxygen and hydrogen—Its reproduction by explosion of mixed gases—Solar heat rendered latent in separated oxygen and vegetable tissue—Its liberation by combustion of vegetable tissue in air—All terrestrial force traceable to the sun—Accumulation of solar force by vegetable organisms—Its dissipation by animal organisms—Reverse subsidiary actions—Baseless hypothesis of vital force—Artificial performance of alleged vital syntheses—Stages of constructive vegetal and destructive animal action—Occurrence of same intermediate products in both kingdoms—General processes of synthetic chemistry—Passage from one organic group to next in complexity—Continuous series of synthetic operations—Production of urea, formic acid, prussic acid, trimethylamine, and chloroform from mineral elements—Synthesis of di-carbon compounds, including alcohol, taurine, acetic acid, glycocine, and oxalic acid—Of tri-, tetra-, and penta-compounds, including glycerine, the lactic, butyric, succinic, malic, tartaric, and valeric acids, and fousel oil—Of hexa-compounds, including caproic acid, leucine, and grape sugar?—Of hepta-compounds, including oil of bitter almonds, and the benzoic, salicic, and gallic acids—Possible artificial manufacture of food.

(68.) At the conclusion of my last lecture I was insisting upon the importance of viewing the phenomena of animal and vegetable life in relation to the external forces of the universe. I observed that, however valuable might be the study of the more minute and elementary forms of life, and I was far from wishing to decry its value in any way, there were, on the other hand some great truths which could only be appreciated by comparing the most highly specialised forms of life with one another, not in their minute details, but in their broad general features. I also observed, that while the chief cosmical function of highly-developed vegetable life was deoxidation, or the separation of oxygen from carbon and hydrogen, the leading function of highly developed animal life was oxidation—the recombination of the separated oxygen and carbo-hydrogen with one another; and we agreed to consider upon this occasion the essential nature of these two correlative processes. I said, further, that I was induced to bring this subject under your notice in a more elementary and detailed manner than I originally contemplated, from finding that certain principles believed by physicists to be as fundamental as the laws of gravitation were not heartily and unreservedly admitted by physicians.

(69.) First of all, then, we have to inquire into the character and import of that deoxidation of carbonic anhydride and water, which takes place in vegetable organisms, and the origin of the forces by which it is brought about. Now, in entering upon the discussion of this question, I must direct your attention for a short time to topics which at first sight seem but very remotely connected either with chemistry or physiology. To paraphrase in sober earnest the expressions used in sarcasm by a very distinguished Fellow of this College, the value of whose contributions to physiological science no one can be more ready than myself to acknowledge, I shall preface my remarks by a few observations upon force and the constancy of its amount in the universe. Then, by a reference to systems and suns, and worlds, and steam-engines, and mills, and telegraphs, I shall endeavour to satisfy you that the same forces are at work in living plants and animals as in the inorganic world; and that the study of the indestructibility and correlation of force will teach us much, though far indeed from all, concerning the nature of life.

(70.) Let us begin, then, by considering the correlation that exists between the forces of heat and motion—their equivalency with, and convertibility into, one another—of which no better illustration perhaps can be chosen than a steam-engine; and the philosophical toy upon the table, known as Hero's œlipile, will answer our purpose perfectly well. On lighting a fire under the boiler of a steam-engine, some of the heat liberated in the furnace gradually passes into the water; and as each successive increment of heat is absorbed from the furnace, the temperature of the water rises until it arrives at a certain point. During the time the water takes in rising from its original temperature up to the boiling point, heat is being conveyed into it, at what may be regarded as an uniform rate. When, however, a certain degree of heat is reached, the temperature of the water no longer rises, although the heat of the furnace continues passing into it at the same rate as before; but now, some of the heat absorbed, instead of being manifested in the form of heat, appears in the form of motion, and the steam-engine begins to work. Just as in the œlipile before you, the heat of the spirit-flame was passing into the water for several minutes with no other effect than that of raising its temperature; whereas, after the lapse of several minutes, the heat of the flame still passing into the water ceased to increase its temperature in the slightest degree, but caused instead a rapid rotatory motion of the instrument. Thus, we perceive generally that the development of motion is consequent upon an absorption of heat, and conversely, we shall find that an arrest of motion is tantamount to the liberation of heat. For example, if we employ our steam power in drilling a piece of metal, the motion of the engine is lessened by the friction of the drill, and a certain amount of heat is thereby generated. The original heat of the furnace, absorbed by the boiling water without any increase of its temperature, produces a less amount of motion than formerly, but the diminution of motion is supplemented by a remote increase of heat—less of the heat which passes into the water being now manifested in the form of motion, but the difference reappearing at a distance in its primitive form of heat.

(71.) Similarly when a bullet strikes upon an iron target, its motion is suddenly arrested, and its temperature as suddenly raised. That which was motion has become heat, and the quantity of heat shared between the bullet and the target is exactly proportional to the previous velocity of the bullet, or to the quantity of its motion that has been arrested. Again, in exact proportion to the diminution of motion in the working parts of the steam-engine, so is the amount of heat developed by the friction of the drill upon the piece of metal. For not only are heat and motion convertible into one another in a general way, but they are convertible in a manner which admits of accurate measurement. By suitably contrived experiments it may be shown, in every instance, that so much heat developed is equivalent to so much motion arrested, and conversely that so much motion generated is equivalent to so much heat absorbed. It has been ascertained for instance, more particularly by Mr. Joule, that the force of a pound weight falling through 772 feet is exactly equal to the amount of heat which a pound of water will give out in cooling one degree Fahrenheit; or, in other words, that the heat developed by the arrest of the motion of a pound weight falling through 772 feet would raise the temperature of a pound of water one degree, and that the heat given out by the cooling of a pound of water one degree would lift a pound weight to the height of 772 feet. Heat and motion, therefore, are in every case interchangeable for one another according to a definite standard of equivalency.

(72.) Now, let me direct your attention to some simple illustrations of motion; and, first of all, to the direct motion of a projectile hurled from the arm of a man. Upon seeing the rapid flight of a dart or javelin through the air, we recognise immediately that the motion of the javelin did not originate in itself, but was impressed upon it by some external force. We never think of attributing its motion to the exercise of any peculiar javelin force, but to the action of the muscular force by which it was originally projected. We know that the momentum of the javelin is exactly proportionate to the amount of force exerted in hurling it, and that when it strikes some distant object, the blow which that object receives is as surely struck by the man as if he had delivered it directly with his fist. Let us now take an illustration in which motion is transmitted through the intervention of some simple instrument, as in the case of a bow and arrow, for example. Here, also, the motion of the arrow through the air does not take place in virtue of any force originating in the bow, but is consequent on the muscular force exerted in drawing the bow and cord asunder; and, limited only by the susceptibility of the bow, the momentum of the arrow depends entirely upon the amount of force exerted by the archer in pulling the bow-string.

(73.) Again, in discharging a cross-bow, the cord is first drawn over the catch by a muscular effort, and the arrow afterwards projected by the release of the cord. Now, although the susceptibility of this kind of bow is far more limited than that of a long bow, still it is evident that the force with which the arrow is eventually projected does not originate in the bow, but is only a transformation of the muscular force exerted in separating the bow and cord from one another. Moreover, if instead of pulling the trigger of the cross-bow immediately after the cord is drawn over the catch, we allow the bow to remain in its bent state for weeks, or months, or years, and then release the cord; still the force with which the arrow is at last projected will be the original muscular force exerted at the moment of pulling the bow and cord asunder. Suppose, for instance, that I were to draw the cord of a cross-bow over the catch to-day, and a century hence some one were to release it by touching the trigger, still the force of the projected arrow would not be his force, but my force, exerted by me to-day, lodged in the bow for a hundred years, then manifested in the motion of the arrow, and finally transformed into heat upon the cessation of its flight.

(74.) Similarly, the force with which a cannon-ball falling from the top of the Monument would strike the pavement beneath, would be the exact expression of the force exerted in lifting it to the top—that is to say, in separating the cannon-ball and the pavement a certain distance from each other, no matter how many years before. We may thus render muscular force latent in a stretched bowstring, raised cannon-ball, or other instrument, for any length of time. This latent force is generally spoken of as potential energy, while the active force exertable at any moment by the flying arrow or falling ball constitutes its actual or dynamic energy. Thus the actual energy of my arm becomes the potential energy of the crossbow, reappears as the actual energy of the projectile, and is finally not lost, but dissipated in the form of heat. The point, then, I wish particularly to impress upon you is, that the actual mechanical energy manifested in the falling together, or springing together, of two separated bodies, the ball and the earth, the cord and the bow, is only a liberation of the potential energy stored up in them at the moment they were pulled apart from one another.

(75.) Let us now turn our attention to an altogether different kind of pulling apart, namely, the pulling apart of oxygen and hydrogen from their state of chemical combination. I am here repeating the well-known experiment of the electrolytic decomposition of water. By means of a galvanic battery I am tearing asunder the previously combined oxygen and hydrogen, and collecting the two gases in separate cylinders. Now, what is the nature of this separation, and how is it brought about? Seizing one link in the chain of actions as a starting-point, let us consider first of all the combustion of zinc in the battery-cell; for in all ordinary batteries the direct or indirect oxidation of zinc is the source of the power obtained. Upon holding this bundle of loose zinc shavings in the blowpipe flame, you see that the metal takes fire from time to time and burns with very great brilliancy, being converted into the white flocculi of oxide of zinc which are now floating about the room. If we introduce the ignited zinc into a vessel of chlorine, it continues to burn, you observe, with even greater intensity than before, producing abundant fumes of chloride of zinc. But we may obtain chloride of zinc more readily by dissolving the metal in hydrochloric acid; and in this case, also, the combination of zinc with chlorine is attended by an evolution of heat. Thus, the solution of granulated zinc in hydrochloric acid, now taking place in this gas-generating flask, is being accompanied by a considerable elevation of temperature in the liquid, as well as by an evolution of hydrogen, according to the equation—

Zinc		Hydrochloric		Zinc chloride		Hydrogen
Zn''	$+$	$2HCl$	$=$	$Zn''Cl_2$	$+$	H_2.

(76.) Now, equivalent for equivalent, the quantity of heat liberated by the combination of zinc with oxygen or chlorine is much greater than that evolved by the similar combination of hydrogen; and accordingly, when we burn zinc at the expense of hydrogen, as in this experiment, we obtain in the flask just so much of the heat produced by the burning of the zinc as is in excess of the heat absorbed in the unburning, so to speak, of the hydrogen.* Hence, leaving out of consideration certain subsidiary phenomena, the heat produced by the solution of a given quantity of zinc in hydrochloric acid, and the heat producible by burning the thereby liberated hydrogen in an atmosphere of chlorine, added together, would exactly equal the amount of heat producible by burning the same quantity of zinc directly in chlorine gas, as we did a minute or two ago. Thus, by the solution of zinc in hydrochloric or sulphuric acid, we have a certain proportion of the combination-heat of the metal set free. The intensity of this heat is not great, in consequence of its being associated with so large a mass of matter in the flask, but

* *Vide* Professor Williamson's lecture ' On the Dynamics of the Galvanic Battery.' *Phil. Mag.* xxvi. 452. Taking as our unit of heat the quantity of heat necessary to raise the temperature of a kilogramme of water $1°$ C. —that is to say, from $0°$ C. to $1°$ C.—it is found that 65 grammes of zinc Zn'', in combining with twice 35·5 grammes of chlorine Cl_2, to form 136 grammes of chloride of zinc $Zn''Cl_2$, evolve 101·31 units of heat; whereas 2 grammes of hydrogen H_2, in combining with twice 35·5 grammes of chlorine Cl_2, to form 73 grammes of hydrochloric acid $2HCl$, evolve only 47·56 units of heat. Hence in decomposing 73 grammes of hydrochloric acid by 65 grammes of zinc, according to the equation $Zn'' + 2HCl = Zn''Cl_2 + H_2$, we should have 101·31 − 47·56 = 53·75 units of heat liberated as initial battery power.

DERIVATION OF GALVANIC FORCE. 73

its quantity is very considerable, and constitutes, indeed, the entire dynamic energy we have at our disposal in the galvanic battery.

(77.) When the zinc and platinum plates of the battery communicate freely with each other, the combination-heat of the attacked zinc is manifested solely by a rise of temperature in the contents of the cell, precisely as in the case we have just considered of the simple solution of granulated zinc in hydrochloric acid. But the battery is a machine for enabling us to apply and transform this combination-heat of the zinc in a variety of ways. For instance, if I complete the communication between the zinc and platinum plates by means of a platinum wire, you observe that the small coil of wire assumes an intense state of ignition. Now, the heat of this platinum wire is nothing more than a portion of the translated heat of the zinc burning in the cell; which, instead of being manifested at the point of action in the cell, is manifested at a distance in the wire; much as a portion of the furnace heat absorbed in the evaporation of water may be manifested at a distance by the friction of a drill. The heat exhibited by the platinum wire does not originate in the wire, but in the cell, and so much of the heat of the burning zinc as appears in the wire is lost to the cell. Just as the contracting muscle strikes its blow at a distance of many yards by means of the conducting javelin, so does the burning zinc strike its blow at the spot whereto it is conducted by the copper strands.

(78.) In electro-motive machines, the heat of the burning zinc is employed in doing mechanical work, just as the heat of burning coal is employed, though with far greater economy, in a steam-engine. But in the decomposition of water taking place upon the table, the heat of the burning zinc is employed in the chemical work of pulling oxygen and hydrogen apart from one another. Of the heat producible by the combustion of a given weight of zinc, the proportion manifested externally in the ignition of platinum wire, or employed externally in the separation of oxygen and hydrogen, is supplemental to the quantity absorbed in heating the cell; so that in the electrolysis of water, as in the heating of platinum wire, so much the more external work done, so much the less internal heat developed. By the electrolytic decomposition of water, the heat of the burning zinc, which does not appear internally in the cell, and which might be manifested externally in the ignition of platinum wire, lies dormant in the separated oxygen and hydrogen; but it is not lost. On the contrary, I can render it evident to you with the greatest ease. Now that we have collected a sufficient quantity of our electrolytic gases, I have only to mix them together and explode them, when you observe a considerable evolution of light and heat resulting from their combination; which light and heat are nothing more than the light and heat of the burning zinc, not manifested in the cell, but retained for a time in the separated gases, so as to constitute their potential energy. The explosion of the gases at once or a hundred years hence would make no difference. The heat and light resulting from their eventual explosion would still be the heat and light of the burning zinc stored up in them, so to speak, at the moment of their electrolysis. In my last lecture I showed you the formation of water by the combustion of hydrogen in the oxygen of the air, and called your attention specially to the heat developed by the combination. The heat so developed did not originate in the oxygen and hydrogen, but was simply a liberation of the heat force, which, directly or indirectly, at some time or other, had been employed in pulling them apart, and been rendered latent in them so long as they continued apart—just as the force of a stretched cross-bow does not originate in the bow, but is merely latent muscular force stored up in the separated bow and cord. Similarly in the brilliant combustion of carbon in oxygen gas to form carbonic anhydride, there was no generation of heat, but only a liberation of the heat previously stored up in the two separated elements.

(79.) At length, then, we are in a position to understand the nature of the action taking place in the vegetable kingdom, by which carbonic anhydride and water are decomposed—to consider what is the external force employed in the pulling apart of oxygen from hydrogen and carbon, and what becomes of it. This force is no other than the light and heat force emanating from the sun, rendered latent in the oxygen on the one hand, and the carbo-hydrogen of vegetable tissue or secretion on the other, and reproducible by the act of their recombination or combustion. The sun's rays, for instance, falling upon the leaves of the sugar-beet or sugar-cane effect an eventual decomposition of carbonic acid into oxygen and sugar, thus:—

Carb-anhydride	Water	Sugar	Oxygen
$12\ CO_2$ +	$11\ H_2O$ =	$C_{12}(H_{22}O_{11})$	+ O_{24}

But the heat and light of the sun absorbed in this pulling apart of oxygen and carbon, the one discharged into the atmosphere, the other retained in the vegetable juices, are not lost, but rendered latent in the oxygen and sugar respectively. Here I have a mixture of sugar with a compound in which the oxygen of the air has been accumulated, namely, chlorate of potassium, and on touching the mixture with a drop of sulphuric acid—on pulling the trigger of the cross-bow, so to speak—there is produced a violent deflagration, in which the light and heat of the sun, stored up in the separated sugar and oxygen, are again manifested to you by the combination of the two bodies with one another to reproduce carbonic acid. The light and heat of this combustion, and, indeed, of every combustion, are nothing more than the light and heat of the sun, originally absorbed by the living plant, and rendered latent in the tissue of the plant, and oxygen of the air respectively. Even the heat evolved by the direct or indirect combustion of zinc is no exception; it is only the heat stored up in the metal at the moment of its deoxidation by means of the coal or charcoal in which the sun's force was intermediately retained.

(80.) We see, then, in this way, that the vegetable organism is a machine in which the sun's energy is absorbed in the pulling apart of carbon and hydrogen from oxygen. The light and heat force emanating from the sun is rendered latent in the separated oxygen and carbo-hydrogen, just as human muscular force is rendered latent in the stretched cross-bow. When the separated carbo-hydrogen, in the form of some vegetable product, is recombined with the evolved oxygen, as in burning coal and wood upon the fire, or in consuming bread and oil and wine in the animal frame, the heat liberated in both instances is nothing more than the heat of the sun which had been stored up in the carbo-hydrate and oxygen respectively. Conversely, the animal frame is a machine in which the sun's energy is set free by the recombination of that oxygen and carbo-hydrate, in the pulling apart of which it had been absorbed or rendered latent. The plant may be regarded as a miser, or hoarder up; the animal, on the other hand, as a spendthrift, or dissipator, of the sun's force; but just as the miser is not a producer, or the spendthrift a destroyer of gold, so neither is the vegetable a producer, nor the animal a destroyer of force. All modern philosophy combines to prove that force, like matter, is indestructible. It may be accumulated, but not created; be dissipated, but not destroyed. The force of every kind, active or latent, existing in the earth, at any given moment, is only the sum of the force received by the earth from the sun in excess of the force radiated back from the earth into space.

(81.) Hitherto, in contrasting the functions of animal and vegetable life with one another, I have had regard to their broad general features, looking at each description of life as a whole. A more detailed examination, however, shows us that oxidising and deoxidising processes are common to both kingdoms of nature. For instance, the germination of seeds and maturation of fruits are strictly oxidising, while the conversions of starch and sugar into fat in the animal organism, are strictly deoxidising or vegetative acts. It would seem, indeed, that in all purely nutritive processes, whether of vegetable or animal life, there is an absorption or rendering latent of force, and consequent necessity for its extraneous supply. In highly-developed vegetable life this force is derived directly from the sun. In highly-developed animal life it is obtained by a liberation, within the body, of the sun's force which had been rendered latent in the food we eat and air we breathe respectively. But whilst nutrition, or the storing up of force, constitutes the chief action of vegetable life, in animal life it occupies an altogether subordinate position. For the prime characteristic of animality is activity, the employment of pent-up force in the production of external acts. Hence, while in the vegetable and animal organism, deoxidising and oxidising processes, constructive and destructive actions alike take place, in the vegetable the destructive are subordinate to the constructive, whilst in animals the constructive are subordinate to the destructive acts.' The contraction, for instance, of a man's muscle depends entirely upon the oxidation or destruction of the substance of that muscle, and the equivalent of motion produced upon the amount of muscle destroyed.

(82.) Thus we perceive that all actions of the animal body are traceable to cosmical force; that in living as in dead matter there is no creation of force; and that any explanation of the phenomena of life which recognises the agency of vital force is simply no explanation at all. Applying the word force as we now do to certain transferable states of actual or potential activity having quantitative metamorphic correlations, I much question whether the expression chemical force is a correct one, though it is one of which the meaning is perfectly definite and intelligible. By the chemical force of so much oxygen and hydrogen, for instance, we mean the potential energy stored up in them at the moment of their separation, and reproducible from them in the act of their combination. Similarly, we might apply the phrase vital force to the potential energy of so much fat or muscle, capable by oxidation of being manifested in the form of external heat or motion. But what the physiologist means by vital force I have never been able to understand. So far as I can make out, it seems to be a sort of internal, intransferable, immeasurable, self-originating power, which performs nutritive acts by its absolute will and pleasure; as if it were not abundantly manifest that the growth of a plant and incubation of an egg cannot be performed without a direct supply, and the development of animal organisms without an indirect supply of external force. Speaking of the progress of natural science, Mr. Mill has very pertinently observed that for a long time 'fictitious entities continued to be imagined as means of accounting for the more mysterious phenomena; above all, in physiology, where under great varieties of phrase, mysterious *forces* and *principles* were the explanation, or substitute for explanation, of the phenomena of organised beings.'

(83.) Seeing, then, that the enormous number and variety of animal and vegetable compounds are produced out of carbonic acid, water, and ammonia, not by any peculiar vital force, but merely by the light and heat force of the sun acting through organic machinery, the question naturally arises whether the chemist may not effect in his laboratory-machinery a similar intercombination of deoxidised carbonic acid and water, either by a direct application of sun-force, or, indirectly, by the aid of those terrestrial transformations of sun-force which are so abundantly at his disposal. This question, decided absolutely, in the negative so long as the fiction of vital force tyrannised over men's minds, has of late years received a rapid succession of brilliant affirmative replies. Already hundreds of vegetable compounds heretofore produced only in living organisms, and, as was supposed, put together and held together by vital force, have been formed by the chemist in his laboratory out of carbonic acid, water, and ammonia, or, in other words, out of charcoal, hydrogen, oxygen, and nitrogen. That a still greater number of compounds have not been so formed is due more to a deficiency of knowledge than of power; for as our acquaintance with the constitution of bodies, and with synthetic processes, is daily advancing, so is the unlimited constructive power of chemical art becoming daily more and more apparent.

(84.) Before proceeding, however, to exemplify this power of forming organic compounds artificially, I will first make one or two further remarks upon the order of their natural production. At present we are unable to trace the series of changes, undergone by carbonic acid and water, which result in the formation of tartaric acid, or sugar, or fat, or other complex vegetable product.

FORMATION OF VEGETABLE PRODUCTS. 79

It seems probable, however, that the process by which such bodies are constructed does not consist in the simultaneous deoxidation of several atoms of carbonic acid into one complex molecule, as illustrated by the equation used in my last lecture to explain the production of mannite,—

Carb-anhydride		Water		Oxygen		Mannite
6 CO_2	+	7 H_2O	−	13 O	=	$C_6H_{14}O_6$;

but that a series of more and more complex, less and less oxidised, intermediate bodies are successively produced, by the fixation of deoxidised carbonic acid upon the previously formed compounds. For example, we may conceive mannite to be built up somewhat in this manner. By a simultaneous dehydration and deoxidation of two molecules of carbonic acid, we should first obtain oxalic acid, thus:—

2 Carbonic acid				1 Oxalic acid
$C_2H_4O_6$	−	(H_2O + O)	=	$C_2H_2O_4$

Then by a further deoxidation of oxalic and carbonic acids, we might obtain tartaric acid, thus:—

1 Oxalic acid	$C_2\ H_2\ O_4$
2 Carbonic acid	$C_2\ H_4\ O_6$
	$C_4\ H_6\ O_{10}$
4 Oxygen	O_4
Tartaric acid	$C_4\ H_6\ O_6$

Lastly, by a joint deoxidation of tartaric acid, carbonic acid, and water, we might obtain mannite, thus:—

1 Tartaric acid	$C_4\ H_6\ O_6$
2 Carbonic acid	$C_2\ H_4\ O_6$
2 Water	$H_4\ O_2$
	$C_6\ H_{14}O_{14}$
8 Oxygen	O_8
Mannite	$C_6H_{14}O_6$

The actual occurrence of these particular actions is quite unproven; but that some such actions take place is rendered highly probable by a variety of considerations. Thus, in the gradual development and ripening of the olive, we find certain vegetable acids replaced by mannite, and at a later stage this mannite itself replaced by the less oxidised and more complex oleine. (De Luca.)

(85.) Again, the compounds formed in one organ of a plant are known to be transferred, in a more or less altered form, to other organs, in which they become accumulated; and it is not improbable that certain vegetable products of deoxidised carbonic acid and water may have undergone a partial reoxidation, or even several alternate reoxidations and deoxidations, in the course of their history. Similarly in animals, although the ultimate process is one of oxidation, we know that in certain proximate principles of food the oxidation of some of their constituents is effected at the expense of the remainder, which consequently became deoxidised; and it is possible that some animal products may have undergone an entire deoxidation, or even several alternate deoxidations and reoxidations, before their final discharge from the body. On all these points very much yet remains to be learned; but still, the general position holds good, that vegetables effect a simultaneous deoxidation and intercombination of carbon molecules, while animals conversely effect their simultaneous reoxidation and separation. In many instances, also, the representatives of certain stages of building up and breaking up, in vegetable and animal life respectively, are closely allied to, or even identical with, one another. Oxalic acid, for instance, the simplest product of vegetable synthesis, and a frequent constituent of both the highest and lowest vegetable organisms, may be formed, as we have just seen, by a deoxidation of carbonic acid. But it also occurs abundantly in animal juices and secretions, not as a product of the deoxidation of carbonic acid, but as the last intermediate stage in the oxidation or downward transformation of more complex bodies into carbonic acid; just as the oxalic acid of commerce is obtained from sugar by a process of oxidation which, if carried too far, yields little else than carbonic acid. Benzoic acid, again, which enjoys a wide distribution in the vegetable kingdom as a product of deoxidation, is also a constant result of the natural and artificial oxidation of animal tissues. The power, then, of producing such bodies as benzoic acid and oxalic acid out of more complex bodies such as albumin and sugar, by artificial processes of oxidation, more or less similar to the natural processes taking place in the animal body, has for a long time past been in the acknowledged possession of the chemist. Now, I propose to furnish you with illustrations of his inverse power, to which I have so often referred, of producing both animal and vegetable compounds by deoxidising, or synthetic, or vegetative processes—that is to say, of forming organic compounds without having any recourse to living organisms or reputed vital forces.

(86.) I will first give you an account of the general processes employed for passing from a more simple to a more complex group, and then of the particular processes by which certain individual substances have been obtained, interspersing occasional remarks upon the nature and relationship of some of the substances themselves. At starting, let me recall to your recollection the associated series of homologous fatty acids and alcohols, as written up on the table before you:—

Alcohols		Acids	
$C H_4 O$	Methylic	$C H_2 O_2$	Formic
$C_2 H_6 O$	Ethylic	$C_2 H_4 O_2$	Acetic
$C_3 H_8 O$	Propylic	$C_3 H_6 O_2$	Propionic
$C_4 H_{10} O$	Butylic	$C_4 H_8 O_2$	Butyric
$C_5 H_{12} O$	Amylic	$C_5 H_{10} O_2$	Valeric
$C_6 H_{14} O$	Caprylic	$C_6 H_{12} O_2$	Caproic
$C_7 H_{16} O$	Anthylic	$C_7 H_{14} O_2$	Œnanthic
$C_8 H_{18} O$	Octylic	$C_8 H_{16} O_2$	Thetic

Now, by a variety of processes, some new, some old, it is, and for a long time past has been, possible for us to fasten on to one or other of these alcohols an additional atom of carbon, in such a way as to produce the acid corresponding to the alcohol next in the series. Thus, by means of prussic acid CHN, or carbonic anhydride CO_2, or phosgene $COCl_2$, we can convert methyl-alcohol into acetic acid, vinic alcohol into propionic acid, propyl-alcohol into butyric acid, and so on; but until very lately we could not step from acetic to propionic acid, or from propionic to butyric acid,—that is to say, we could obtain butyric acid $C_4H_8O_2$, from certain members of the 3-carbon group, but not from those members which we had ourselves produced from the 2-carbon group; and, similarly, we could produce propionic acid $C_3H_6O_2$, from certain members of the 2-carbon group, but not from those members which we had ourselves produced from the 1-carbon group. The series of synthetic operations by which it would be possible to pass from any group not merely to the next, but to the next but one, and so on *ad libitum*, was incomplete through our ignorance of the metamorphic relation subsisting between the acid and its associated alcohol. The alcohol, and not the acid, being the plastic member of the group, we could convert the 1-carbon alcohol into the 2-carbon acid, and the 2-carbon alcohol into the 3-carbon acid, and so on; but being unable to convert the 2-carbon acid into the 2-carbon alcohol, we could not by any means pass from the 1-carbon to the 3-carbon group. Very recently, however, this difficulty has been overcome by the separate researches of Wurtz and Mendius, who have shown us how to transform any acid into its corresponding alcohol; whereby a continuous series of synthetic processes may now be carried on as far as we please. Without entering into purely chemical details, I may say that the process of Wurtz consists in transforming the aldehyd of the acid into the normal form of the alcohol; while that of Mendius consists in transforming the nitrile of the acid into the ammoniated form of the alcohol, by means of nascent hydrogen, as illustrated below in the case of ethylic alcohol, thus:—

Aceto-nitrile			Ethyl-amine
C_2H_3N	$+ \ H_4$	$=$	C_2H_7N or $C_2H_5.H_2N$

Acet-aldehyd			Ethyl-hydrate
C_2H_4O	$+ \ H_2$	$=$	C_2H_6O or $C_2H_5.HO$

			Ethyl-chloride
—	—		C_2H_5Cl or $C_2H_5.Cl$

The amine is readily convertible into the hydrate, and the hydrate into the chloride, bromide, or iodide; which last bodies, or their metal derivatives—such, for example, as sodium-ethylate $C_2H_5.NaO$, and sodium-ethyl $C_2H_5.Na$—are the forms of alcohol most usually employed in actual synthetic processes.

(87.) Prior, then, to this discovery by Wurtz and Mendius, of means for passing from the acid to its alcohol by hydrogenation, although many important syntheses had been effected, there had been no consecutive series of syntheses. The previously known processes would allow us to pass from certain mobile members or one group to certain immobile members of the next, but would carry us no further. Nowadays, however, by transforming the immobile acid into the mobile alcohol, we can proceed continuously through an apparently unlimited series of synthetic operations. Thus, letting CO stand for the transferable part of carbonic anhydride CO_2, phosgene-gas $COCl_2$, and aqueous prussic acid $CHN.H_2O$, we have the following series of operations leading to the production of fatty acids and alcohols of any degree of complexity, each of them capable of metamorphosis into scores of allied compounds; which, again, are capable of entering into combination with one another, as explained in my second lecture, to form still more numerous and complicated polymerone bodies.

		Methylic				Acetic		
1-Carb. alcohol		CH_4O	+	CO	=	$C_2H_4O_2$		
		Acetic						Ethylic
2-Carbon acid		$C_2H_4O_2$	+	H_4	=	H_2O	+	C_2H_6O
		Ethylic				Propionic		
2-Carb. alcohol		C_2H_6O	+	CO	=	$C_3H_6O_2$		
		Propionic						Propylic
3-Carbon acid		$C_3H_6O_2$	+	H_4	=	H_2O	+	C_3H_8O
		Propylic				Butyric		
3-Carb. alcohol		C_3H_8O	+	CO	=	$C_4H_8O_2$		
		Butyric						
4-Carbon acid		$C_4H_8O_2$	&c. &c.					

Starting from the 1-carbon or methyl-alcohol, we can convert it into the 2-carbon or acetic acid by well-known processes. But in order to proceed from the 2-carbon acid, we must first transform it into the 2-carbon alcohol—the alcohol, in some or other of its forms, being the synthetic starting-point, so to speak—and this we have very recently learned to do. Then, by affixing deoxidised carbonic anhydride on to the 2-carbon alcohol, we convert it into the 3-carbon or propionic acid. Then by acting upon propionic acid by deoxidised water, we transform it into 3-carbon or propyl-alcohol, upon which we again affix deoxidised carbonic anhydride to convert it into the 4-carbon or butyric acid, and so on continuously, by a series of deoxidising actions with carbonic oxide and hydrogen alternately.

(88.) Now let us proceed to notice briefly, in the order of their complexity, some of the more interesting organic or carbon compounds which have been produced artificially by elementary synthesis. Among mono-carbon compounds, we have first carbonic acid CH_2O_3, alike the most important product of animal oxidation and subject of vegetable deoxidation. Associated with carbonic acid or hydrate, we have carbonic amide or urea CH_4N_2O, a body standing towards carbonic acid in the same relation that ammonia stands to water, and convertible into carbonic acid by an exchange of certain elements of ammonia for the corresponding elements of water, thus :—

Urea	Water	Ammonia	Carbonic acid
$(CO)''H_4N_2$ +	$(H_2)H_2O_2$ =	$(H_2)H_4N_2$ +	$(CO)''H_2O_2$

Carbonic acid is likewise met with in its dehydrated form as carbonic anhydride CO_2, and as the sulphur derivative of that body or carbonic sulphide CS_2. These compounds are obtainable by burning charcoal in oxygen and sulphur respectively, the last of them, under the name of disulphide of carbon, being now produced on an enormous scale for certain manufacturing uses. Moreover, by the dehydration of carbonic acid, a substance that is known only in the state of solution, we also produce carbanhydride, as shown in the following equation—

SYNTHESIS OF FORMIC ACID. 85

Carbonic acid		Water		Carb-anhydride
CH_2O_3	−	H_2O	=	CO_2

which is reconvertible into the acid or a salt thereof by actual or potential rehydration, thus:—

Carb-anhyd.		Lime		Chalk
CO_2	+	$Ca''O$	=	$CCa''O_3$

Carb-anhyd.		Potash		Potas. bicarb.
CO_2	+	KHO	=	$CKHO_3$

The deoxidised forms of carbonic acid and anhydride, respectively, or formic acid CH_2O_2, and carbonic oxide CO, are readily procurable therefrom by processes of reduction, and are correlated with each other in a similar manner. For example, by the dehydration of formic acid, we obtain carbonic oxide,

Formic acid		Water		Carb. oxide
CH_2O_2	−	H_2O	=	CO ;

convertible into a formiate by means of caustic alkali, thus:—

Carb. oxide		Potash		Potas. formiate
CO	+	KHO	=	$CKHO_2$

(89.) The production of formic acid or formiates by the reduction of carbonic acid with sodium (Kolbe), and by the combination of potash with carbonic oxide (Berthelot), being among the early examples of the formation of organic from inorganic compounds, excited on their first announcement a large amount of chemical interest. Formic acid, indeed, is a substance enjoying a very extensive natural distribution. In the vegetable kingdom it occurs in the juice of the stinging nettle, in decaying pine needles, and as a product of the spontaneous oxidation of turpentine. In the animal kingdom it has been occasionally recognised in human blood, urine, perspiration, and in the fluids of the spleen and muscles. It also exists largely in the juice of red ants, from which it may be obtained by simple distillation, and in the corrosive fluid of certain caterpillars, &c. Again, by combining formic acid with ammonia, we obtain formiate of ammonia, which yields by dehydration that important organic compound met with in cherry-laurel water, bitter almond emulsion, &c., and known as prussic acid, cyanide of hydrogen, or formionitrile, thus:—

Formic acid		Ammonia		Water		Prussic acid
CH_2O_2	+	H_3N	−	$2H_2O$	=	CHN

Moreover, this acid, or a corresponding cyanide, may nowadays be procured, not only from formic acid, but by the direct combination of carbon, nitrogen, and a metal.

Further, by oxidising a cyanide—that of potassium CKN, for instance—we obtain cyanate of potassium CKNO, convertible by double decomposition into cyanate of ammonia, which changes spontaneously into urea, thus:—

Ammonia cyanate		Urea
$CHNO.H_3N$	=	CH_4N_2O

This is the celebrated reaction by which urea was first produced artificially by Wöhler in 1828; but, at that time, the cyanogen of the cyanide of potassium employed was known only as a product of organic origin. You observe that by oxidising formic acid CH_2O_2, we obtain carbonic acid; and by oxidising the monammoniated form of formic acid—namely, prussic acid CHN,—in presence of more ammonia, we obtain the di-ammoniated form of carbonic acid—namely, urea; which has since been produced by several other artificial processes.

(90.) The still less oxidised monocarbon compounds belong to the methyl sub-group, and are, principally—

Methyl Compounds

{ CH_4	or	$CH_3.H$	Methyl-hydride or marsh-gas
{ CH_3Cl	or	$CH_3.Cl$	Methyl-chloride
CH_4O	or	$CH_3.HO$	Methyl-hydrate or wood-spirit
CH_5N	or	$CH_3.H_2N$	Methyl-amine

These four bodies—the methyl varieties of hydrogen, hydrochloric acid, water, and ammonia—are mutually convertible by a variety of processes. Marsh-gas, in addition to its occurrence as the chief constituent of coal-gas, as the fire-damp of coal mines, and as the gas of stagnant ponds or marshes, has recently been recognised by Pettenkofer as a normal ingredient of expired air. Wood-spirit, again, is not only a product of destructive distillation, but occurs in nature as a constituent residue of the essential oil of wintergreen, thus:—

Wintergreen-oil	Water	Salicic acid	Wood-spirit
$C_8H_8O_3$ +	H_2O =	$C_7H_6O_3$ +	CH_4O

Among other well-known methyl-compounds may be mentioned sarcosine, kreatine, caffeine or theine, theobromine, coniine, narcotine, &c. &c. Methylamine I have already referred to on several occasions. Associated with it we have trimethylamine $(CH_3)_3N$, a frequent constituent of stale brine in which herrings and other fish have been pickled.

(91.) The production of methylic from carbonic or formic compounds may be effected in a variety of ways. Thus, prussic acid, by hydrogenation, yields methylamine:—

Prussic acid	Hydrogen	Methylamine
CHN +	H_4 =	CH_5N

Formiate of barium is decomposed by heat with production of marsh-gas, thus:—

Barium formiate	Barium carb.	Carb-anhyd.	Marsh-gas
$2\left\{\begin{array}{l}CH\\CH\end{array}\right. Ba''\begin{array}{l}O_2\\O_2\end{array}$ =	$2CBa''O_3$ +	CO_2 +	CH_4

Marsh-gas also results from passing a mixture of carbonic sulphide and sulphuretted hydrogen over metallic copper heated to redness, thus:—

Carb. sulph.	Hyd. sulph.	Copper	Cupr. sulph.	Marsh-gas
CS_2 +	$2H_2S$ +	Cu_8 =	$4Cu_2S$ +	CH_4

Perhaps a still more interesting mode of obtaining methyl-compounds consists in submitting disulphide of carbon to prolonged treatment with chlorine gas, whereby it is converted into perchloride of carbon, which by the continuous action of nascent hydrogen yields the following series of compounds:—

Marsh-gas Derivatives

$C\ Cl_4$	Perchloride of carbon
$CH\ Cl_3$	Chloroform
CH_2Cl_2	Dichloromethene
CH_3Cl	Chloride of methyl
CH_4	Methene, or marsh-gas

Thus, among monocarbon compounds of purely artificial production, we have the following interesting bodies, of which all save the last occur naturally in the vegetable or animal kingdom, namely, urea, formic acid, prussic acid, trimethylamine, and chloroform.

(92.) The principal members of the dicarbon group, namely, alcohol and acetic acid, together with their respective congeners, are procurable from monocarbon compounds by a variety of processes. Thus, according to some observations of my own, on submitting a mixture of marsh-gas and carbonic oxide to a full red heat, acetylene or klumene is produced, thus,—

Marsh-gas		Carb. oxide		Water		Klumene
CH_4	$+$	CO	$=$	H_2O	$+$	C_2H_2 ;

and this klumene, when acted upon by nascent hydrogen, yields olefiant gas, or ethylene, thus:—

Klumene		Hydrogen		Ethylene
C_2H_2	$+$	H_2	$=$	C_2H_4

Now, olefiant gas, as pointed out by Faraday and Hennel nearly fifty years ago, and as rediscovered and established beyond question by Berthelot within the last few years, is absorbed by oil of vitriol, and upon distilling the diluted acid, is liberated therefrom in the form of alcohol or spirit of wine, thus:—

Ethylene		Water		Alcohol
C_2H_4	$+$	H_2O	$=$	C_2H_6O

This production of alcohol from olefiant gas, or ethylene, an important constituent of ordinary coal gas, is undoubtedly, in many points of view, a result of very great interest, but as a step in organic synthesis I think its importance has been somewhat over estimated—alcohol and olefiant gas being closely allied members of the same carbon group. However, Berthelot's discovery of a process for obtaining alcohol by purely inorganic means naturally achieved considerable notoriety, and gave a great impetus to the general prosecution of synthetic methods.

(93.) You observe that artificial alcohol is produced from olefiant gas, which is itself produced from acetylene or klumene, which is itself produced from monocarbon compounds of strictly mineral origin. But a still more interesting way of obtaining acetylene has also been rediscovered and established by Berthelot, namely, the combustion, so to speak, of carbon in hydrogen gas. When charcoal is burnt in oxygen, the heat evolved by the initial combination is more than sufficient to maintain the combustion, and accordingly the piece of charcoal when once ignited continues to burn. But in the combustion of charcoal in hydrogen, if it may so be called, the piece of charcoal has to be maintained throughout in an intense state of ignition by means of the electric arc. When, for instance, the charcoal terminals of a moderately powerful battery, enclosed in a globe through which a current of dry hydrogen is passing, are approximated to each other so as to become ignited, as in the ordinary electric lamp, the hydrogen and ignited carbon combine with one another to form hydride of carbon or acetylene, much in the same way that oxygen and ignited carbon combine with one another to form oxide of carbon or carb-anhydride. But oxidation tends to the separation, hydrogenation to the conjunction of carbon atoms; and accordingly, while by the combustion of charcoal in oxygen we obtain only the monocarbon compound CO_2, by its combustion in hydrogen we obtain the dicarbon compound C_2H_2, which is separated from the excess of hydrogen by transmission through an ammoniacal solution of the white or inferior chloride of copper, whereby it is retained in the form of cuprous acetylide C_2HCu. This compound is thrown down as an abundant bright red precipitate, and, by treatment with warm hydrochloric acid, is decomposed with liberation of acetylene gas, thus:—

Cupr-acetylide	Chlorhyd. acid	Cuprous chlor.	Acetylene
C_2HCu +	HCl =	$CuCl$ +	C_2H_2

Acetylene is characterised by the extreme luminosity with which it burns. You observe the great opacity and whiteness of its flame, and the large amount of light afforded by it in proportion to its bulk, when compared, for instance, with the flame of ordinary coal gas, of which, indeed, acetylene is a constituent, though only to a small extent. By hydrogenising his cuprous acetylide with a mixture of zinc and ammonia, instead of treating it with hydrochloric acid, Berthelot produced olefiant gas or ethylene, from which, by indirect hydration with sulphuric acid, he afterwards obtained alcohol, as I have already described.

(94.) Now, among other animal products, alcohol occurs as a residue of tyrosine, a compound to which I shall refer more particularly in my next lecture; and, as I have before observed, of taurine, which is producible in the following manner:— Under certain circumstances, the residues of alcohol and sulphuric acid combine with one another to form isethionic acid, easily convertible into chlorethyl-sulphurous acid $C_2H_5ClSO_3$, by means of pentachloride of phosphorus. This chloride is retransformable into its hydrate or isethionic acid $C_2H_5(HO)SO_3$, by the action of water, while both the chloride and the hydrate are transformable into the amide or taurine $C_2H_5(H_2N)SO_3$,* by

---

* These formulæ are not meant to express the assumed internal molecular arrangement of the three bodies, but only their positively ascertained mutual relationship.

means of ammonia, according to the following reactions, the first of them due to Kolbe, the second, which is earliest in point of time, to Strecker :—

Chloride and Hydrate					Taurine or Amide
$C_2H_5(Cl)SO_3$	+	$H(H_2N)$	=	HCl +	$C_2H_5(H_2N)SO_3$
$C_2H_5(HO)SO_3$	+	$H(H_2N)$	=	H_2O +	$C_2H_5(H_2N)SO_3$

(95.) Alcohol is also procurable from acetic acid by the hydrogenising processes of Wurtz and Mendius, already described; while acetic acid is reprocurable from alcohol by oxidation, as in the ordinary manufacture of vinegar. Moreover, acetic acid $C_2H_4O_2$, may be obtained synthetically from methyl-alcohol CH_4O, by fixation of carbonic oxide CO, according to the previously mentioned general methods; and also from disulphide of carbon by Kolbe's historic process, referred to in my last lecture. The successive stages of this, the earliest unimpeachable process for obtaining an organic compound by strictly mineral means, are indicated in the table before you —

Acetic Acid Synthesis

CS_2	Carbon disulphide
CCl_4	Carbon tetrachloride
C_2Cl_4	Tetrachlor-ethylene
$C_2HCl_3O_2$	Trichlor-acetic acid
$C_2H_4O_2$	Acetic acid

The disulphide of carbon, produced by the direct combination of sulphur and carbon, is converted, by treatment with chlorine, into tetrachloride of carbon; this, by heating to redness, into tetrachlor-ethylene; this, by the action of moist chlorine, into trichlor-acetic acid; and this, by means of nascent hydrogen, into ordinary acetic acid. By arresting the hydrogenation at a certain point, and treating the so formed monochlor-acetic acid $C_2H_3ClO_2$, with ammonia, we obtain glycocine, whereas by treating it with methylamine we obtain sarcosine, which, in combination with urea, constitutes kreatine, a compound, however, that has not yet been prepared artificially.

Thus, among 2-carbon products of the animal and vegetable kingdom, that have been obtained by strictly mineral processes, may be mentioned alcohol, taurine, acetic acid, glycocine, and last, though not least important, oxalic acid; which results from the oxidation of alcohol, acetic acid, and glycolic acid, &c., and is producible synthetically from the mono-carbon formic and carbonic acids.

(96.) By means of the general processes to which I directed your attention some time back, as well as by certain special processes, it is easy to pass from the 2-carbon to the 3-carbon group, upon which, however, we must rest satisfied with bestowing a very cursory glance. It comprises among its members glycerin $C_3H_8O_3$, the basic principle of the true fats, whether of vegetable or animal origin. Also lactic acid $C_3H_6O_3$, an important constituent of the juice of flesh, and a product of that fermentation of grape-sugar and milk-sugar which is set up by putrefying curd. We have also the chief constituents of essential oil of garlic, or allyl-sulphide $(C_3H_5)_2S$, and of essential oil of mustard, or allyl-sulphocyanate $(C_3H_5)H.CNS$, to be included in the list of artificially produced members of the propionic family.

(97.) Passing on to the 4-carbon group, we have first butyric acid $C_4H_8O_2$, a product of the destructive metamorphosis of sugar, mannite, &c. Combined with alcohol it forms butyric ether or essential oil of pine-apple, while combined with glycerin it forms that constituent of ordinary butter which is known as butyrin. Succinic acid $C_4H_6O_4$, is readily procurable from butyric acid, and bears to it the same relation that oxalic bears to acetic acid. It is probably the most frequent artificial product of the oxidation of fatty matters, and has also been met with naturally in the cystic fluids of hydatids, hydrocele, &c. From succinic acid it is easy to procure in succession the well-known vegetable products, malic acid $C_4H_6O_5$, and tartaric acid $C_4H_6O_6$, which, again, are reconvertible into succinic acid. The malic and succinic acids, in particular, are very intimately associated with, and readily convertible into, one another. Thus, asparagine $C_4H_8N_2O_3$, the crystalline principle of asparagus and other etiolated plants, yields one or other of these acids, according to the treatment to which it is subjected.

(98.) The 5-carbon compounds of artificial origin are of less general interest. I may mention fousel oil or amyl-alcohol $C_5H_{12}O$, and valerianic or valeric acid $C_5H_{10}O_2$, a product originally obtained from essential oil of valerian. By combining amyl-alcohol with acetic acid we procure the pear flavour, and by combining it with valeric acid, the apple or quince flavour used in confectionery, which are probably identical with the essential oils existing naturally in the ripe fruits. Again, by combining valeric acid with glycerin we produce valerin, a constituent of whale oil.

(99.) Of the 6-carbon fatty compounds which have been artificially obtained, the most interesting are caproic acid $C_6H_{12}O_2$, and leucic acid $C_6H_{12}O_3$. Caproic acid is met with as a glyceride in goat's butter, while amido-caproic acid or leucine is an occasional constituent of human urine, and a constant product of the metamorphosis of glandular tissue. Starch $C_6H_{10}O_5$, grape sugar $C_6H_{12}O_6$, mannite $C_6H_{14}O_6$, and a host of allied alimentary substances are also included in this group, though their exact relationship to the typical members is not as yet clearly established. Now, grape sugar has been obtained by Berthelot from glycerin, which is itself, as I have said, obtainable by purely inorganic means; so that, in one sense, sugar may be added to the list of artificially produced organic compounds. Still the means employed for effecting the conversion of the glycerin—namely, the action of putrefying animal tissue—must prevent our regarding the resultant sugar as being strictly of inorganic origin; although formed exclusively out of the glycerin, the animal tissue not having contributed any actual material to its formation. However, if sugar has not yet been obtained by a satisfactory process, the recent production of strictly allied bodies, such as the propyl-phycite of Carius, together with our increasing knowledge of the metamorphic relations of sugar itself, assures us that an unexceptionable means for building up this important alimentary principle cannot much longer escape us.

Hitherto the transformation of fatty into aromatic compounds has not been accomplished according to any definite reaction; but both phenene C_6H_6, and phenol or carbolic acid C_6H_6O, are producible by transmitting the vapour of alcohol or fousel oil through red-hot tubes. From the former of these bodies we readily obtain aniline or phenylamine C_6H_7N, which is reconvertible into both phenene and phenol.

(100.) The 7-carbon fatty acid and alcohol are usually obtained from castor oil. So far as I know, they have not yet been produced artificially from inorganic materials, but undoubtedly could be so produced at any moment. With the 7-carbon aromatic compounds the case is different. By the general processes already referred to, phenene has been converted into benzoic acid $C_7H_6O_2$, by Harnitzky and Kekulé, and phenol into salicic acid $C_7H_6O_3$, by Kolbe. Benzoic acid readily yields benzoic aldehyd or essential oil of bitter almonds, and also glycobenzoic or hippuric acid. Salicic acid, again, is readily oxidisable into gallic acid, of which tannin constitutes the natural glucoside, as shown by the following decomposition:—

Tannin		Water		Glucose		Gallic acid
$C_{27}H_{24}O_{17}$	+	$4H_2O$	=	$C_6H_{12}O_6$	+	$3C_7H_6O_5$

From salicic acid we may also obtain methyl-salicate or essential oil of wintergreen, salicic aldehyd or essential oil of spiræa, and saligenin or salicylic alcohol, a compound frequently mentioned in my second lecture as a constituent residue of salicin and populin—salicin being, indeed, a glucoside of saligenin, much in the same way that tannin is a glucoside of gallic acid, thus:—

Salicin		Water		Glucose		Saligenin
$C_{13}H_{18}O_7$	+	H_2O	=	$C_6H_{12}O_6$	+	$C_7H_8O_2$

Moreover, tyrosine — a very remarkable product of· tissue metamorphosis—though not yet produced from salicic acid, has much the same relation thereto that leucine has to caproic, and sarcosine and glycocine have to acetic acid—it being, indeed, the ethyl-ammoniated form of salicic acid.

Another 7-carbon compound of artificial production, and of great interest in an industrial point of view, is benzoene, or toluol C_7H_8, which Fittig and Tollens have recently obtained from phenene or benzol C_6H_6. Starting from these two bodies, we may procure all the so called coal-tar colours, with the brilliancy and variety of which most of us are now familiar. The red base or rosaniline $C_{20}H_{19}N_3$, the violet base or triethyl-rosaniline $C_{26}H_{31}N_3$, and the blue base or triphenyl-rosaniline $C_{38}H_{31}N_3$, being producible in this way from their constituent elements, furnish us with admirable illustrations of the constructive powers of modern organic chemistry.

(101.) Thus have I illustrated to you the mode in which chemists can nowadays, without any recourse to vitality, build up primary molecules containing as many as seven atoms of carbon, either from carbonic acid, water, and ammonia, the materials out of which living organisms construct identical or similar molecules, or else from the elementary substances, carbon, hydrogen, oxygen, and nitrogen, upon which living organisms can exert no plastic action whatever. I might even proceed further, but should then be obliged to depart from the regular sequence I have hitherto followed. Moreover, my object has been rather to illustrate to you the general mode of procedure than to make known to you the utmost limits that have as yet been attained. Of the three great classes of alimentary substances, the oleaginous are quite, and the saccharine almost within our reach. The albuminous, indeed, are still far beyond us; and no wonder, since their very constitution is at present not only unknown, but unsuspected. In their case, however, as in that of many other bodies, so soon as we succeed in unravelling the mystery of their natural composition, so soon may we aspire confidently to the work of their artificial reconstruction.

(102.) Only a few words more, which I will borrow from my friend Dr. Frankland, who has himself contributed very largely to synthetic methods and results. 'It would be difficult,' said he, 'to conclude a subject like the present without some notice of the considerations which naturally suggest themselves regarding the possibility of *economically* replacing natural processes by artificial ones in the formation of organic compounds. At present, the possibility of doing this only attains to probability in the case of rare and exceptional products of animal and vegetable life. By no processes at present known could we produce sugar, glycerin, or alcohol from their elements at one hundred times their present cost, as obtained through the agency of vitality. But, although our present prospects of rivalling vital processes in the economic production of staple organic compounds, such as those constituting the food of man, are exceedingly slight, it would be rash to pronounce their ultimate realisation impossible. It must be remembered that this branch of chemistry is as yet in its merest infancy; that it has hitherto attracted the attention of but few minds; and further, that many analogous substitutions of artificial for natural processes have been achieved. . . . . In such cases where contemporaneous natural agencies have been superseded, we have almost invariably drawn upon that grand store of force collected by the plants of bygone ages and conserved in our coal-fields.'

LECTURE V.

Muscular action dependent on muscular metamorphosis—Theoretic oxidation of muscle into one proportion of urea and seven of carbonic acid—Practical results—Dynamic value of muscle oxidation—Quantities of heat producible by combustion of hydrogen and carbon—Difference between quantity and intensity of heat—Unit of heat equivalent to 424 kilogrammetres of motion—Quantities of motion producible by combustion of hydrogen and carbon—Economy of muscle as a motive exponent of combustion—Reciprocity of heat and motion in muscular action—Solar origin of muscular force—Amount of force derivable from muscle proportional to degree of its oxidation—Imperfect knowledge of natural process of oxidation—Artificial oxidation of muscle—Nature of intermediate products—Relation of aldehydes and nitriles to acids—Simple constitution of acids obtained by muscle oxidation—Production of both fatty and aromatic compounds—General distribution of leucine and tyrosine—Their formation by indirect oxidation of nitrogenous tissue—Leucine the most elaborate of fatty, and tyrosine of aromatic animal products—Constitution and analogies of leucine or amido-caproic acid—Probable constitution of tyrosine, or ethylamido-salicic acid—Natural history of salicic compounds, including indigo—Occurrence in human urine of indigo, salisuric acid, and phenol—Relationship of tyrosine to hippuric acid.

(103.) THAT muscular exertion is dependent on muscular metamorphosis or oxidation is a subject rather for the physiologist than the chemist to dilate upon. Perhaps, however, I may be permitted to remind you of such observations as the following—that a free supply of thoroughly oxygenated arterial blood is essential for complete well-developed muscular action; that the volume of oxygen contained in blood which has circulated through a contracting muscle is less than one-fourth of that contained in blood which has traversed the same muscle at rest,

H

while there is a corresponding increase, not of course an equal increase, in the volume of its carbonic acid; that the irritability of muscular fibre out of the body is arrested by its removal from oxygen, and again manifested on its re-exposure thereto; and lastly, that other things being equal, the amount of urea excreted by the kidneys, and of carbonic acid excreted by the lungs, is proportionate to the muscular activity of the individual. Seeing, then, that muscular exertion is really dependent upon muscular oxidation, we have to consider what should be the products, and what the value of this oxidation.

(104.) Unfortunately, the precise molecular formula—the exact chemical constitution—of muscle is at present unknown. But in muscle, as in all the albuminoïd class of bodies, we do know the ratio in which the constituent carbon and nitrogen stand to one another. Thus it is established beyond all question that the ratio of the number of atoms of carbon to the number of the atoms of nitrogen in muscle is as nearly as possible, if not quite exactly, four to one. In the most minute fragment of muscle, then, for every single atomic proportion of nitrogen there are four atomic proportions of carbon, thus:—

4 Carbon to 1 Nitrogen.

It will be more convenient, however, to express this ratio by the doubles of the above numbers, so that, instead of four to one, we will adopt eight to two, as our expression of the atomic ratio of carbon to nitrogen in every particle of muscle:—

8 Carbon to 2 Nitrogen.

Admitting, further, as a result of its ultimate metamorphosis, that the whole of the nitrogen of muscle is converted into urea, let us first consider what proportion of its carbon must be associated with this nitrogen to produce urea, and what proportion be thereby left for excretion in the form of carbonic acid. Now, although the molecular constitution of muscle is undetermined, that of urea is perfectly definite.* As shown by its formula, CN_2H_4O, the molecule of urea consists of one atom of carbon, two atoms of nitrogen, four atoms of hydrogen, and one atom of oxygen. In other words, leaving out of consideration its hydrogen and oxygen, the atomic ratio of nitrogen to carbon in urea is as two to one. Accordingly, every two atoms of nitrogen in urea have one atom of carbon associated with them; so that if we take the two proportions of nitrogen existing in muscle and add to them the one proportion of carbon necessary to form urea, we shall have seven proportions of carbon left for conversion into carbonic acid, thus:—

$$7 \text{ Carbon to } \begin{cases} 1 \text{ Carbon} \\ 2 \text{ Nitrogen} \end{cases}.$$

The theoretical result, then, of the complete oxidation of muscle is the appearance of one-eighth of its carbon in the form of urea, and of seven-eighths of its carbon in the form of carbonic acid.

(105.) Now, let us see what is the actual result. We have two series of experiments made by Bischof and Voit, and Pettenkofer and Voit respectively, in which lean dogs were fed exclusively upon a moderate diet of flesh. In the first series of experiments a small proportion of fat left in the flesh was duly allowed for; while in the second series the fat was entirely removed. The general results of the two series of experiments are shown below:—

C. of Carb. acid		C. of Urea	
7·29	to	1	Bischof and Voit
6·85	to	1	Pettenkofer and Voit
7·07	to	1	Mean

Thus the ratio of carbon excreted in the form of carbonic acid to carbon excreted in the form of urea was as 7·29 to 1 in the

* This mode of viewing the relationship of muscle to urea and carbonic acid was suggested by Dr. Lyon Playfair's essay 'On the Food of Man in relation to his Useful Work,' to which I am otherwise much indebted in the early part of this lecture.

first series of experiments, as 6·85 to 1 in the second series, and as 7·07 to 1 in the mean of the two. Theoretically, then, the ratio of carbon in carbonic acid to carbon in urea is as 7 to 1; experimentally it is found to be as 7·07 to 1—a striking mutual corroboration of the two methods of calculation and research.

(106.) With regard to the dynamic value of muscle oxidation, I told you in my last lecture that, by the separation of oxygen from carbon and hydrogen, a certain amount of heat-force was absorbed and rendered latent in the separated bodies, which, by their re-combination, was again liberated and rendered sensible. Confining our attention to hydrogen, and speaking in round numbers, we may say that the heat evolved by burning a cubic foot of hydrogen—that is, by combining a cubic foot of hydrogen with half a cubic foot of oxygen—will raise the temperature of $5\frac{1}{2}$ cubic feet of water one degree Fahrenheit; or that the heat of burning hydrogen is capable of raising the temperature of $5\frac{1}{2}$ times its bulk of water one degree. But, seeing that the quantity of matter in a body is proportionate to its weight, we get a much better idea of the amount of heat developed, by comparing the items gravimetrically instead of volumetrically. We thus find that the combustion of one part by weight of hydrogen will evolve an amount of heat sufficient to raise the temperature of more than 61,000 parts of water one degree Fahrenheit, or 34,000 parts of water one degree centigrade. Now, in comparing the amounts of heat given out by the combustion of different substances, it is convenient to have some definite standard of comparison; and the usual continental standard is altogether, perhaps, the most convenient. According to this standard, the amount of heat given out by one kilogramme of water in cooling one degree centigrade, or, conversely, the amount of heat absorbed by one kilogramme of water in rising one degree centigrade, is called the unit of heat. We find, then, that when one gramme of hydrogen gas is burned into water, it gives out 34 units of heat; or it will raise the temperature of 34 kilogrammes—that is, 34,000 times its own weight—of water one degree; while, turning our attention to carbon, we find that one gramme of carbon, in being oxidised or burned into carbonic anhydride, gives out 8 units of heat, or will raise the temperature of 8 kilogrammes—that is to say, 8000 times its own weight—of water one degree.

(107.) It must be remembered, of course, that the quantity of heat evolved during the oxidation of a given weight of hydrogen, carbon, or other combustible, is perfectly independent of the rapidity or slowness of the action. Provided only that the same products are formed, the same amount of heat is liberated in their formation, whether it takes place rapidly or slowly, violently or gradually. It is only the intensity of the heat, and not its quantity, which varies with the rapidity of the combination. When a stout piece of iron rusts in the air, we get oxide of iron produced as the result of the slow burning of the metal, but there is no obvious rise of temperature. On the other hand, when a piece of iron wire is burned in oxygen gas, we have a brilliant combustion, and an intense development of heat. In reality, the products formed in these two cases are not identical, but only allied. Assuming them, however, to be identical, the amount of heat given out in the rapid burning of the metal would be identical with that given out during its slow rusting. The difference is merely that in the one case all the heat is given out in the course of a few seconds—that there is a great quantity of heat produced in a short time—while in the other case this same quantity of heat is developed only during a long series of years. As a matter of fact, the quantity of heat evolved by the slow rusting of a given weight of iron is considerably greater than that evolved by its rapid combustion in oxygen, the resulting compound being not only more highly oxidised, but in a state of hydration, or combination with solid water.

(108.) A very ordinary experiment will serve, perhaps, to illustrate more strikingly the point now under consideration. Upon immersing this plate of copper in a jar of chlorine gas, for instance, the chlorine combines gradually with the metal, and there is no evident rise of temperature; but when very thin copper leaf is immersed in chlorine gas, the combination takes place instantaneously, with evolution of sufficient heat to render the leaf luminous—with vivid combustion, in fact—as you perceive. Now, the amount of heat given out under these opposite circumstances is identical; the only difference is in its intensity —in the quantity of heat associated with a given quantity of matter at a given moment. In the last case, the action being instantaneous, and the quantity of matter to be heated very small, we have what we call an intense heat—that is, the momentary association of a large quantity of heat with a small quantity of matter; whereas in the other case, the action being gradual, the development of heat is likewise gradual, spread over a long period of time, and associated with a large quantity of matter, the increased temperature of which is, therefore, at no one moment very perceptible. The terms quantity and intensity of heat are strictly analogous to the terms quantity and velocity of motion. In a pound weight of iron raised to $1000°$—the melting point of silver,—or ten pounds weight raised to $100°$—the boiling point of water,—the quantity of heat capable of being imparted—say, to a gallon of ice-cold water—is substantially the same, though the intensity of the heat is ten times as great in the one case as the other; just as the quantity of motion is the same in a pound weight moving at the rate of 1000 feet, or a ten-pound weight moving at the rate of 100 feet per second, although the velocity of motion is ten times as great in the one case as the other. We come, then, to this conclusion—that chemical action, whether rapid or slow, provided only that the same substances react and the same products result, always furnishes the same amount of heat.

(109.) Now, let us apply this fundamental law of combination to the fuel-constituents of our tissues. If we inflame a mixture of hydrogen and oxygen gases, the combination and consequent evolution of heat being instantaneous, we obtain, indeed, the highest degree of temperature capable of being produced by direct chemical action. On the other hand, if we take the same mixture of oxygen and hydrogen gases, and cause them to unite slowly by means of spongy platinum, the oxidation and development of heat being spread over a period of many minutes, there is no great manifestation of temperature at any one instant. The quantity of heat is, however, the same in both cases. One gramme of hydrogen in combining with oxygen, whether quickly or slowly, will always evolve 34 units of heat; and one gramme of carbon in combining with oxygen, whether quickly or slowly, will always evolve 8 units of heat. The slow oxidation of so much carbon and hydrogen in the human body, therefore, will always produce its due amount of heat, or an equivalent in some other form of energy; for while the latent force liberated by the combustion of the carbon and hydrogen of fat is expressed solely in the form of heat, the combustion of an equal quantity of the carbon and hydrogen of voluntary muscle is expressed chiefly in the form of motion. You may remember that I referred in my last lecture to the equivalency subsisting between heat and motion—to the circumstance that so much heat was convertible into so much motion. Accordingly, when we burn or oxidise the carbo-hydrogen of animal tissue, instead of getting the heat-force which was exerted in separating this carbo-hydrogen from oxygen remanifested in the form of heat, we have it, under certain circumstances, manifested in the form of motion.

(110.) Let us then proceed to consider what are the quantitative relations subsisting between heat and motion. We have taken as our unit of heat the quantity of heat absorbed or evolved by one gramme of water in rising or falling through one centigrade degree of temperature. Now, this is found by experiment to be the exact quantity of heat generated by collision with the earth of a kilogramme weight falling from a height of 424 metres. So that the mechanical force of a kilogramme weight which has fallen through 424 metres, or, in other words, the mechanical force necessary to lift a kilogramme weight to the height of 424 metres, is equal to, interchangeable for, and convertible into the heat-force evolved or absorbed by a kilogramme of water in changing its temperature one degree. Or the arrest of a unit of motion would raise the temperature of a kilogramme of water at zero one degree, and conversely, the absorption of a unit of heat would lift 1 kilogramme weight to the height of 424 metres. Of course, the force necessary to lift 1 kilogramme through 424 metres, or 10 kilogrammes through 42·4 metres, or 424 kilogrammes through 1 metre, is the same; whence it is convenient to apply the expression kilogram-metre to the product of the kilogrammes lifted into the metres of height, and to say that the heat evolved by the cooling of a kilogramme of water one degree centigrade is equal to 424 kilogrammetres of motion, and *vice versâ*. Or we may adopt Mr. Joule's original standard, and say that the heat evolved by the cooling of a pound of water one degree Fahrenheit is equal to 772 foot-pounds of motion.

(111.) The applicability of these considerations to the combustions of hydrogen and carbon taking place in the animal body is obvious. We have said that the combustion of 1 gramme of hydrogen evolves 34 units of heat, and that a unit of heat is equal to 424 kilogrammetres of motion; so that the combustion of 1 gramme of hydrogen will produce $34 \times 424 = 14{,}416$ kilogrammetres of motion; or will serve to lift 1 kilogramme weight through 14,416 metres of height, or 14,416 kilogrammes through 1 metre of height, &c. &c. Similarly, the combustion of 1 gramme of carbon will suffice to produce 3392 kilogrammetres of motion, thus:—

One gramme burnt				Kilogrammetres of motion
HYDROGEN	34	×	424 =	14,416
CARBON	8	×	424 =	3,392

In this way, then, we can form some idea of the mechanical power generated, or quantity of motion producible, by the combustion of the hydrogen and carbon of our muscles into water, and carbonic acid or urea respectively.* Our knowledge of the

---

* The heat produced by the conversion of carbon into urea is doubtless that producible by its complete burning into carbonic anhydride CO_2, and not merely that producible by its half burning into carbonic oxide CO, as sometimes represented.

intimate constitution of muscle is, however, too imperfect to allow of our estimating the amount of motion producible by its oxidation with any degree of exactitude; but, as the result of a rough calculation, it may be taken that the combustion of the unburnt carbo-hydrogen of one gramme of dry muscle, free from fat, is capable of furnishing 1923 kilogrammetres of motion, or will suffice to lift 1923 kilogrammes to the height of 1 metre.*

(112.) Now, although the ratio of the [amount of motion actually produced to that theoretically producible by the combustion of a given weight of muscle, has not, I believe, been satisfactorily ascertained, this much is certain,—that muscular tissue is, without exception, by far the most perfect of machines for manifesting the force liberated by chemical action in the form of motion. No artificial contrivance with which we are acquainted is at all comparable to it in economy—that is to say, in the proportion of mechanical work performed to the total force liberated. The steam-engine, for instance, is an artificial machine, expressly intended for the conversion of chemical force into motion. Heat is generated in the boiler-furnace by a combination of the carbo-hydrogen of the coal with the oxygen of the air, but only a certain amount of this heat is absorbed in the evaporated water, and then only a certain amount of the heat so absorbed is translated into motion. According to Sir W. Arm-

* Assuming for muscle the formula $C_{12}H_{19}N_3O_4 \times 6$, and subtracting all the oxygen and nitrogen, with the necessary hydrogen, in the forms of water and ammonia, so as to leave a residue of $C_{12}H_2 \times 6$, then 269 grammes of muscle would leave 144 grammes of carbon and 2 grammes of hydrogen for oxidation, which should furnish 517,280 kilogrammetres of motion, thus:—

	Grammes		Kilogrammetres		Kilogrammetres
CARBON	144	×	3,392	=	488,448
HYDROGEN	2	×	14,416	=	28,832
					517,280

Hence one gramme of muscle should furnish 517,280÷269=1923 kilogrammetres of motion; but from the imperfection of the data on which the calculation is based, particularly as regards the heat absorbed in the separation and volatilisation of carbon, this result can only be regarded as approximative.

strong, indeed, not more than one-tenth of the force liberated by the combustion of the coal used for raising steam is realised as available motion. Be this as it may, it appears that by burning, or consuming, or oxidating a given weight of muscle in our bodies, we obtain a quantity of available motive force which could only be produced by the combustion of at least five or six times its weight of coal in the most perfect steam-engine that ever was constructed.

(113.) The superior economy of muscle over any artificial contrivance, as a motive machine, seems to depend in great measure upon the circumstance of the force liberated by its oxidation being expressed directly in motion, instead of first appearing in some intermediate form of energy. Thus, in a steam-engine, the immediate effect of the oxidation is not motion, but heat, some of which eventually or intermediately appears as external motion. In this case, the combination first produces heat, and the heat is afterwards transformed into motion; whereas, in muscular tissue, the combination first produces motion, which is afterwards, in many cases, transformed into heat. The force liberated by the combustion of the muscular fibre of the heart, for instance, is expressed directly in the contraction of its ventricles, and the consequent propulsion of the blood through the greater and lesser circulations. But by the time the blood gets back to the heart, it has given up all its motion, and requires to be again propelled by another contraction of the ventricles, and so on. Now, what becomes of the motion received by the blood at each contraction? It appears in the form of heat. The blood circulating through the vessels and capillaries undergoes a certain amount of friction. It is brought to a state of rest gradually by the hindrance to its motion, just as a bullet is brought to rest suddenly by the hindrance to *its* motion. In both cases, that which was motion becomes heat, and, in the latter case, the quantity of heat finally produced by the friction of the blood is generated as truly by the combustion of the heart-fibre, as if it had been burnt directly in a furnace. Under certain circumstances, indeed, as in the attempt to lift a heavy weight, the oxidation of muscle within our bodies produces a direct liberation of heat instead of motion. In the case of a person actually lifting a weight, the combustion of his tissue is expressed in the motion of the weight; but supposing he only attempts to lift a weight which is too heavy for him, there is then no production of motion, but instead of it a corresponding increase of temperature in the muscle. In tetanus, again, where the violent contraction of the muscles produces no external motion, their temperature has been observed to rise as much as six degrees centigrade or eleven degrees Fahrenheit above the normal state. Conversely, in the case of a man working a treadmill, although the amount of heat evolved from his person is absolutely larger, its proportion, relatively to the amount of tissue burned, is smaller than in the case of a person at rest, by a difference equivalent to the external work performed. But in fever, where there is a rapid destruction of tissue without any corresponding mechanical effect, we have a complementary manifestation of external heat.

(114.) Thus we return once again to the conclusion which I brought more prominently under your notice in my last lecture. We perceive that muscular exertion does not result from vital force generated within the body, or, indeed, from force of any kind generated within the body, but only from a liberation within the body of pent-up solar force, which at some time or other had been rendered latent in the separated carbo-hydrate of our food on the one hand, and oxygen of our breath on the other. As ingeniously observed by Dr. Tyndall, when speaking of the sun,—' It is at his cost that animal heat is produced, and animal motion accomplished. Not only is the sun chilled, that we may have our fires, but he is likewise chilled that we may have our powers of locomotion.' From the terms in which I lately referred to the fiction of vital force, some physiologists who honoured me by their presence seemed to infer that chemists and physicists were insensible to those important distinctions existing between living and dead matter, which they, on the other hand, profess to explain by declaring the former to be possessed, and the latter dispossessed, of vital force. I believe, however, that chemists appreciate in its fullest extent what may be termed the mystery of life, but they look upon the physiologists' explanation as a mere periphrasis,—as only another mode of saying that dead matter differs from living matter because it is dead, while living matter differs from dead matter because it is alive. Chemists and physicists are well assured that, be life what it may, it is not a generator, but only a transformer, of external force. In the vegetable kingdom solar force is absorbed in the production of our food; in the animal kingdom it is liberated by the eremacausis of our fat and glands and muscles.

(115.) Now, the full realisation of the force derivable from a given weight of muscle depends upon its complete oxidation into water and carbonic acid or urea. Should it be only converted into sugar, or kreatine, or uric acid, these are imperfectly burned substances, which still retain a certain amount of potential energy liberable from them by a further oxidation. They still have associated with them some portion of the latent force put into the original tissue-constituents at the period of their formation; and accordingly, by their further oxidation, we are capable of getting an additional amount of work out of them. In order, therefore, to obtain the full equivalent of heat-force or motive force to which we are entitled by the waste of our tissues, it is important that this waste should be thorough, that both the hydrogen and carbon should be converted into the most completely oxidised compounds they are susceptible of forming,—the whole of the hydrogen into water, and the whole of the carbon into its most stable monocarbon compound, namely, carbonic acid, or the ammoniated form of that acid, namely, urea. In some cases of imperfect oxidation, however, we get less oxidised, and more complex, dicarbon molecules produced, such, for example, as oxalic acid, which occurs either in its normal saline state, or colligated with urea in the forms of allantoine, oxaluric acid, &c. In cases of yet more imperfect oxidation, we meet with still less oxidised tricarbon molecules, such, for example, as the mesoxalic compound which, by its colligation with urea, forms uric acid. We may even have tetracarbon molecules such as succinic acid, pentacarbon molecules such as amido-valeric acid or phocine, hexacarbon compounds such as amido-caproic acid or leucine, and heptacarbon compounds such as the benzoic residue of hippuric acid, and the salicic residue of tyrosine.

(116.) You will remember that by certain processes of artificial oxidation to which I referred in a former lecture, we obtain from any particular substance a series of less and less complex bodies terminating in carbonic acid; or, to use again the words of Gerhardt, we gradually descend the scale of complexity, converting the original substance into more and more simple products by successively burning off a portion of its carbon and hydrogen. In other cases, however, as in some of Gorup-Besanez's experiments upon the oxidation effected by ozone in alkaline liquids, whether or not a series of bodies intermediate between the initial substance and final carbonic acid are really formed, we are quite incapable of detecting them, and consequently, of tracing their metamorphoses. The constituent carbon-atoms of the original substance seem, at any rate, to become at one step completely isolated and oxidised. Whether, therefore, the more complex molecules formed by natural tissue-oxidation are to be regarded as direct, but intermediate, products of the principal oxidation, or as by-products resulting from subsidiary processes, is at present an open question, though the balance of evidence with regard to certain products, at any rate, seems to be in favour of the latter view. In any case, however, the formation and even excretion of some or other of these bodies, in greater or less proportion, according to the nature of the organism,—uric acid largely in birds and land-reptiles, hippuric acid largely in herbivora, and both acids sparingly in mankind—are obviously normal or healthy actions. By the excretion of such imperfectly burned substances, indeed, a certain amount of force does not become utilised within the animal, but this prodigality of force in organic nature is far inferior to that which we observe in the inorganic world. Some of these intermediate products of tissue metamorphosis, more particularly the hippuric and uric acids, leucine and tyrosine, are of sufficiently constant occurrence and general interest to deserve our special examination. Hippuric acid we have already discussed somewhat fully, while the consideration of uric acid I must postpone to my next lecture. There remain, then, only leucine and tyrosine; but, before adverting to the natural occurrence of these bodies in the living and dead body, let me direct your attention for a short time to certain allied products obtainable from nitrogenous tissue by artificial processes.

(117.) When flesh, for instance, is submitted to the action of the oxidising agent most commonly employed by chemists—namely, a mixture of sulphuric acid with either bichromate of potassium, or peroxide of manganese—there are produced a considerable number of monobasic acids, to which I shall refer more particularly hereafter, together with several of their associated aldehydes and nitriles. Now the relationship of an aldehyd to its corresponding acid and alcohol is very simple, and may be exemplified by common or vinic aldehyd among fatty, and by benzoic aldehyd among aromatic compounds. Thus, when vinic alcohol is submitted to oxidation, it does not simply take up an additional dose of oxygen, but instead gives up a portion of its hydrogen to the oxgenant, being thereby converted into al*cohol* dehyd*rogenatus* or aldehyd, thus:—

Alcohol		Oxygen		Water		Aldehyd
C_2H_6O	+	O	=	H_2O	+	C_2H_4O

The resulting aldehyd is a much more readily oxidisable substance than the original alcohol, and upon exposure to air, is rapidly converted by direct absorption of oxygen into acetic acid, thus:—

Aldehyd		Oxygen		Acetic acid
C_2H_4O	+	O	=	$C_2H_4O_2$

Similarly, benzyl-alcohol is not susceptible of mere oxidation, but, by the action of oxygenants, is dehydrogenised into benz-aldehyd, or essential oil of bitter almonds,—

Benzyl-alcohol		Oxygen		Water		Benz-aldehyd
C_7H_8O	+	O	=	H_2O	+	C_7H_6O

which, upon exposure to air, quickly changes by a direct absorption of oxygen into benzoic acid, thus:—

Benz-aldehyd	Oxygen	Benzoic acid
C_7H_6O +	O =	$C_7H_6O_2$

Oxygen, then, which removes hydrogen from the alcohols, attaches itself directly to the aldehydes, and thereby distinguishes the one class of compounds from the other; even when, as in the case of allyl-alcohol and propionic aldehyd, the two bodies have the same ultimate composition, represented in their case by the empiric formula C_3H_6O.

(118.) Although, however, the characteristic property of the aldehydes is to absorb oxygen with conversion into acids, they may nevertheless be rehydrogenised into alcohols, as by the method of Wurtz referred to in my last lecture, thus:—

Benz-aldehyd	Hydrogen	Benzyl-alcohol
C_7H_6O +	H_2 =	C_7H_8O

Or, still more curiously, one moiety of the reacting aldehyd may be oxidised into the corresponding acid or its salt, and the other moiety simultaneously hydrogenised into the alcohol, as in Cannizzaro's well-known process:—

Benz-aldehyd	Potash	Potas. benzoate	Benzyl-alcohol
$2C_7H_6O$ +	KHO =	$C_7H_5KO_2$ +	C_7H_8O

Correlated, then, with every alcohol and acid is an intermediate aldehyd, several of which bodies, in addition to benz-aldehyd, are familiarly known to us in the form of essential oils. Thus, the essential oils of chamomile, cinnamon, spiræa, and rue, contain the angelic, cinnamic, salicic, and methyl-rutic aldehydes, convertible by oxidation into the angelic, cinnamic, salicic, and rutic acids respectively. The prime characteristic then of the aldehydes is their acidifiability by direct absorption of oxygen; so that, considered as products of oxidation, they may be looked upon as incompletely formed acids. When, therefore, we find that by treating muscle with some oxidising agent we obtain certain aldehydes together with their corresponding acids, it only shows that our oxidising agent is employed in deficiency, or rather that the products, being readily volatile, are not left in contact with the heated oxidising mixture sufficiently long to be entirely converted into acids.

(119.) But in addition to aldehydes and acids, certain nitriles, more particularly formio-nitrile and valero-nitrile, have been obtained by muscle oxidation. You may remember that I have already, in previous lectures, made mention of prussic acid, cyanide of hydrogen, or formio-nitrile; of cyanide of methyl, or aceto-nitrile; of cyanogen, or oxalo-nitrile, &c. The majority of these nitriles are procurable either by the action of the simplest organic nitrile, namely, prussic acid, upon the preceding alcohol, or by the action of ammonia upon the co-equal acid, with elimination of water, as shown below in the case of valero-nitrile:—

Butyl-alcohol		Prussic acid		Water		Valero-nitrile
$C_4H_{10}O$	+	CHN	−	H_2O	=	C_5H_9N

Valeric acid		Ammonia		Water		Valero-nitrile
$C_5H_{10}O_2$	+	H_3N	−	$2H_2O$	=	C_5H_9N

The first process is a true synthesis, or passage from a lower to a higher carbon group, as explained in my last lecture when speaking of general synthetic methods; while the second is merely a metamorphosis of the acid into its dehydrated ammonia-salt. Now by treatment with caustic alkalies, the several nitriles or organic cyanides absorb water to reproduce ammonia and a salt of the acid to which they respectively appertain, thus:—

Valero-nitrile		Potash		Water		Ammonia		Pot. valerate
C_5H_9N	+	KHO	+	H_2O	=	H_3N	+	$C_5H_9KO_2$

Prussic acid		Potash		Water		Ammonia		Pot. formiate
CHN	+	KHO	+	H_2O	=	H_3N	+	$CHKO_2$

Accordingly, the occurrence of nitriles, in addition to acids and aldehydes, only shows that certain oxidation-products of the carbo-

ACIDS OF FLESH OXIDATION. 113

hydrate constituents of muscle exist partly in combination with an ammonia-residue derived from its nitrogenous constituents, whereby, instead of the normal acids, we obtain, in some cases, their dehydrated ammonia salts; whence it follows that the nitriles, like the aldehydes, do not call for any separate consideration, but may be discussed with their respective acids, of which indeed, they constitute mere varieties.

(120.) The following acids, then, in the state of acids, aldehydes, and nitriles, have been obtained by the oxidation of flesh with a mixture of sulphuric acid and peroxide of manganese,—as now taking place in the retort upon the table:—

Fatty Acids		Aromatic Acids	
$C_6 H_{12} O_2$	Caproic	—	—
$C_5 H_{10} O_2$	Valeric	—	—
$C_4 H_8 O_2$	Butyric	—	—
$C_3 H_6 O_2$	Propionic	$C_8 H_8 O_2$	Toluic?
$C_2 H_4 O_2$	Acetic	$C_7 H_6 O_2$	Benzoic
$C H_2 O_2$	Formic	$C_6 H_4 O_2$	Collic?

These several acids, you observe, contain but two atoms of oxygen in their respective molecules. In reality, however, we cannot doubt that corresponding acids with three and four atoms of oxygen are also formed, as in other modes of oxidation; but such poly-oxygen acids being much less volatile than their di-oxygen congeners, instead of being removed at once from the oxidising mixture, remain in contact with it for so great a length of time—are subjected in fact to such a prolonged process of oxidation—that they become more or less completely destroyed, or, in other words, converted into carbonic acid.

(121.) Now, there are two special points of interest connected with the above lists of muscle-acids, which are arranged, you observe, in the order of simplicity, instead of complexity, as heretofore. The first point to which I would direct your attention is, that even the most complex of them is comprised among the simpler members of its particular series. Thus, while by the direct or indirect oxidation of fat we may obtain acids

I

with eight, nine, ten, and even sixteen atoms of carbon, the most complex acids as yet obtained by the artificial oxidation of flesh, are those with five, six, and seven atoms; for the production of toluic acid is at any rate very doubtful. Now, although this oxidation of flesh has not been performed with sufficient frequency, or variety of process, to warrant our laying much stress upon the results obtained, still less of affirming that no more complex aplone molecules than those with seven atoms of carbon are in any case procurable, nevertheless the above observation, taken in conjunction with other facts, has an interest which must not be overlooked. Thus, among all the products of tissue-metamorphosis occurring in the living body, with the possible exception of indigo, which, like toluic acid, contains eight carbon atoms; among all the products of the putrefactive decomposition of dead animal tissue; among all the products obtainable by its direct oxidation as just referred to; and among all the products obtainable by its indirect oxidation with acids or alkalies, not a single aplone molecule with more than seven atoms of carbon has yet been positively observed.

(122.) Comparing the ascertained constitution of olein, for instance, with the hypothetical constitution of some protein body, we know that the molecule of olein contains 57 carbon atoms, and that these atoms pertain to the residues of four distinct aplone molecules, namely, three molecules of oleic acid, containing each 18 carbon-atoms, and one molecule of glycerin, containing 3 carbon-atoms. Accordingly, by the breaking up of olein we may obtain aplone molecules with as many as 18 atoms of carbon, and with successively fewer and fewer atoms, according to the degree of oxidation, until finally we get such bodies as succinic acid $C_4H_6O_4$, oxalic acid $C_2H_2O_4$, and carbonic acid CH_2O_3; while, among intermediate compounds, the palmitic acid with 16, the sebacic and rutic acids with 10, and the suberic acid with 8, are certainly, and other acids with from 1 to 18 carbon-atoms, in all probability, procurable. On the other hand, the composition of the molecule of albumin is at present undetermined; but assuming, according to the balance of authority, that it contains 72 carbon-atoms, what is the number and what the complexity of the aplone molecules between which these 72 carbon atoms are divided? All we can say is that no aplone molecule with more than 7 or 8 carbon atoms has hitherto been produced by its natural or artificial decomposition, so that its constituent residues probably appertain to much simpler molecules, than do the residues of ordinary fat.

(123.) The other point of interest connected with the artificial oxidation of flesh is, that the acids and aldehydes thereby produced belong to both our primary series, namely, the fatty and the aromatic; so that while the oxidation of muscle in the laboratory yields us certain fatty acids which are producible by the similar oxidation of fat, it yields in addition certain acids of the aromatic series that are not producible by the oxidation of fat. This result acquires additional importance from the consideration that chemists are at present quite unable to transform fatty into aromatic compounds, or *vice versâ*, by any definite reaction. It is true that when various bodies of the fatty class are subjected to a full red heat, some products belonging to the aromatic class are formed; but this transformation is one that we cannot trace. It belongs to the class of changes which are termed destructive or indefinite, in contra-distinction to those easily traceable and definite reactions which we call more especially metamorphic. By no ordinary treatment with reagents, and certainly by none of the modes of treatment to which muscle has been subjected, are we able to pass from the fatty to the aromatic class of bodies; and accordingly, when we find, by treating flesh, &c., with sulphuric acid and manganese, that both aromatic and fatty acids are produced, we have a right to infer that, be the exact composition of the flesh what it may, it certainly contains, in addition to its ammonia residues, one or more residues of compounds belonging to the fatty, and one or more residues of compounds belonging to the aromatic class. This conclusion becomes even more irresistible when we consider that not only by the direct oxidation of nitrogenous tissue now taking place on the table, but by its indirect oxidation, through the agency of acids and alkalies, as well as by its post-mortem putrefactive decomposition, and its ante-mortem natural transformation, compounds belonging to both the aromatic and fatty class simultaneously make their appearance.

(124.) Among these compounds, leucine and tyrosine demand our special attention—leucine being an ammoniated term of the 6-carbon fatty, and tyrosine an ethyl-ammoniated term of the 7-carbon aromatic acid group. These two bodies occur in association with one another under the following circumstances: —In the first place, they result from the putrefaction of flesh, cheese, white of egg, gluten of wheat, &c. They have also been detected in fresh blood, and occur very generally in glandular tissue and secretion—leucine, however, in much the larger proportion, so that in some cases where it has been recognised, the tyrosine probably accompanying it has been overlooked. Leucine, more particularly, has been found in the spleen, thymus, thyroid, and lymphatic glands; and, indeed, from its occurrence in the two former, received at one time the names of lienine and thymine. Both compounds are met with most abundantly in the pancreas and its secretion, but they also occur in the liver and bile, and in the kidneys and urine, particularly in certain pathological conditions. Leucine has also been recognised in the salivary and intestinal glands and their secretions, and is, according to Bœdeker, an ordinary constituent of pus.

(125.) That leucine and tyrosine pre-exist in the living body, and are not merely post-mortem products, is evident from the circumstance of their having been detected in the urinary, pancreatic, and, in the case of leucine, purulent and salivary secretions of living animals. But more than this. A long time back, De la Rue noticed that tyrosine existed pre-formed in the dried cochineal insect; and Staedeler, by crushing up various living animals in a mortar with a mixture of powdered glass and alcohol, has recently recognised the presence of both tyrosine and leucine in invertebrata belonging to all the principal non-infusorial classes. Thus it is manifest that leucine and tyrosine are possessed of a very extensive natural distribution. As yet indeed they have not been detected in the juice of flesh, a circumstance which appears the less surprising, however, when we remember that even urea itself, an undoubted product of muscular metamorphosis, has never been satisfactorily recognised in healthy muscular tissue, probably on account of its rapid removal by the circulation.

(126.) Artificially, leucine and tyrosine may be produced not only from flesh, but also from blood-albumin, white of egg, gluten, casein or cheese, gelatin, chondrin, elastic tissue, horn, nails, feathers, hair, hedgehog-spines, cockchafer-elytra, &c. &c., by one or other of two well-known indirect processes of oxidation, which consist respectively in boiling the above-named substances for many hours with some mineral acid, and in fusing them gently with caustic alkali. Now, these two apparently opposite processes are the same in principle. In each case, the acid or alkali merely enables the protein or gelatinoïd substance to react with water H_2O, whereby one portion of it becomes oxidised into leucine, tyrosine, &c., while another portion is hydrogenised into divers products. The nature of this action is best exposed by considering the case of some tolerably simple well-characterised substance—such, for instance, as benz-aldehyd, or essential oil of bitter almonds. When this body is treated with caustic potash, one-half of it becomes oxidised into benzoic acid, which appears in the form of an alkaline benzoate, and the other half is hydrogenised into benzyl-alcohol, as I mentioned a few minutes ago:—

Benz-aldehyd	Water	Benzoic acid	Benzyl-alcohol
$2C_7H_6O$ +	H_2O =	$C_7H_6O_2$ +	C_7H_8O

When, however, a large excess of alkali is used, and the action allowed to become more violent, the hydrogen does not enter into any combination, but is simply liberated in the gaseous state, thus:—

Benz-aldehyd	Water	Benzoic acid	Hydrogen
C_7H_6O +	H_2O =	$C_7H_6O_2$ +	H_2

Now, in fusing the above-mentioned animal substances with caustic alkali, a greater or less proportion of gaseous hydrogen from the decomposed tissue-water is similarly liberated; whereas, in boiling them with mineral acids, the same hydrogen, instead of being liberated, effects certain hitherto unexamined combinations or reactions; while, in both cases, the oxygen of the decomposed water effects the production of leucine and tyrosine. Here are specimens of leucine and tyrosine obtained in this way by the action of sulphuric acid on feathers, and here another fine specimen of tyrosine, extracted from cochineal, all kindly lent me by Dr. Hugo Müller.

(127.) Thus the conclusion that nitrogenous tissue contains a something related to the fatty group and a something related to the aromatic group, suggested by the results of its direct oxidation with peroxide of manganese or chromic acid, is confirmed by the results of its indirect oxidation with acids and alkalies. Among fatty compounds, we obtain, in the one case, caproic acid, and, in the other, amido-caproic acid, or leucine; while among aromatic compounds we obtain, in the one case, benzoic acid, and, in the other, ethyl-amido-salicic acid, or tyrosine. Now, let us consider the constitution and respective relationships of these amidated bodies.

Starting from our primary fatty acids, we may obtain the following series of chlorine derivatives:—

Fatty Acids		α-Derivatives	
$C H_2 O_2$	Formic	$C H Cl O_2$	Chloro-formic?
$C_2 H_4 O_2$	*Acetic*	$C_2 H_3 Cl O_2$	Chlor-acetic
$C_3 H_6 O_2$	Propionic	$C_3 H_5 Cl O_2$	Chloro-propionic
$C_4 H_8 O_2$	Butyric	$C_4 H_7 Cl O_2$	Chloro-butyric
$C_5 H_{10} O_2$	Valeric	$C_5 H_9 Cl O_2$	Chloro-valeric
$C_6 H_{12} O_2$	*Caproic*	$C_6 H_{11} Cl O_2$	Chloro-caproic

Now, if in each of these derived acids we replace the residue of hydrochloric acid, or Cl, by the residue of water, or HO, we obtain a new series of acids; whereas, if we replace it by the residue of ammonia, or H_2N, we obtain a series of amides, thus:—

β-Acids			γ-Amides		
C H (HO)O$_2$		Carbonic	C H (H$_2$N)O$_2$		Carbamic?
C$_2$ H$_3$ (HO)O$_2$		Glycolic	C$_2$ H$_3$ (H$_2$N)O$_2$		*Glycocine*
C$_3$ H$_5$ (HO)O$_2$		Lactic	C$_3$ H$_5$ (H$_2$N)O$_2$		Alanine
C$_4$ H$_7$ (HO)O$_2$		Bulatic	C$_4$ H$_7$ (H$_2$N)O$_2$		Bulatine
C$_5$ H$_9$ (HO)O$_2$		Phocic	C$_5$ H$_9$ (H$_2$N)O$_2$		Phocine
C$_6$ H$_{11}$(HO)O$_2$		Leucic	C$_6$ H$_{11}$(H$_2$N)O$_2$		*Leucine*

Excluding the mono-carbon compounds, whose behaviour in other cases is frequently different from that of their more complex homologues, we find that the β-acids and γ-amides may be obtained from the corresponding fatty acids, through the intervention of their α-chloro-derivatives, as above described. Excluding, again, the mono-carbon compounds, we obtain the β-acids by acting upon the several γ-amides with nitrous acid, whereas by acting on them with an electro-negative chloride and water, we obtain the α-chloro-acids, convertible into the normal acids by treatment with nascent hydrogen. The relation, therefore, of glycocine to the glycolic and chlor-acetic acids, and of leucine to the leucic and chloro-caproic acids, is merely the relation of ammonia H.H$_2$N, to water H.HO, and to chlorhydric acid H.Cl, as I explained to you more fully in my first lecture.

(128.) Glycocine I have referred to on several previous occasions. It is produced, together with leucine and tyrosine, by the action of acids or alkalies upon nitrogenous, and more particularly gelatigenous tissues, whence its original name of sugar of gelatin. It exists as a constituent residue of sarcosine and kreatine, as well as of the hippuric and glyco-cholic acids. The next body, alanine, is obtainable from acet-aldehyd by treatment with aqueous prussic acid in the same way that leucine is obtainable from valer-aldehyd, as mentioned also in my first lecture. By analogy it should be called lactine, were not this appellation otherwise appropriated—namely, by milk-sugar C$_6$H$_{12}$O$_6$, whose formula, you observe, is exactly twice that of lactic acid C$_3$H$_6$O$_3$, a compound to which this sugar is in some way or other very closely related. It is curious that while lactic acid exists so largely in flesh-juice, gastric juice, &c., alanine, which is only an ammoniated form of lactic acid, should never have been recognised in any natural or artificial product of animal tissue. I am not aware that bulatine has yet been obtained from any source whatever; while phocine has been noticed upon one occasion only by Gorup-Besanez in the pancreas of an ox. Leucine, on the other hand, as I have already remarked, exists naturally in, and is producible artificially from, a great variety of animal and vegetable bodies.

(129.) In commencing the study of the constitution of tyrosine, we are at once struck by the great resemblance which its formula bears to that of hippuric acid. You observe that the molecule of tyrosine differs in ultimate composition from the molecule of hippuric acid, by an excess of two atoms of hydrogen, thus:—

$$C_9 H_9 N O_3 \quad \text{Hippuric acid}$$
$$C_9 H_{11} N O_3 \quad \text{Tyrosine}$$

Inasmuch, however, as complex molecules of this description are built up of the residues of several simpler molecules, it may happen, and indeed not unfrequently does happen, that the numbers of the atoms of carbon, hydrogen, oxygen, and nitrogen in two or more complex bodies, approximate very closely to, or are even identical with, one another; whilst the bodies themselves are composed of very different residues, and accordingly have no real relationship of proximate constitution. Such, however, is not the case with hippuric acid and tyrosine. Each of these bodies is composed of three constituent residues—namely, an ammonia residue, a 2-carbon residue belonging to the fatty, and a 7-carbon residue belonging to the aromatic class. That the aromatic residue of tyrosine, however, differs from the residue of hippuric acid in belonging to the salicic instead of the benzoic sub-group, is evident from a variety of considerations pointed out by Schmitt and Nasse, whose recently published views on the constitution of tyrosine, if not demonstrated with absolute certainty, are so probable in themselves, and so supported by collateral testimony, as to leave us in very little doubt as to their substantial correctness. Thus tyrosine agrees with other salicic compounds in the characteristic properties of yielding phenol by distillation, and chloranil by chlorination, and, after suitable treatment, of striking a purple colour with ferric salts, as you perceive. This last reaction constitutes Piria's well-known test for tyrosine. Now, according to Schmitt and Nasse, the particular member of the salicic subgroup which enters into the constitution of tyrosine is salicic acid, whose formula, you observe, differs from that of benzoic acid by an excess of one atom of oxygen. Moreover, benzoic acid is isomeric with salicic aldehyd, and salicic acid with ampelic or oxi-benzoic acid, thus:—

$C_7H_6O_2$ Benzoic acid, and salicic aldehyd
$C_7H_6O_3$ Ampelic acid, and salicic acid

(130.) With regard to the natural history of salicic compounds, salicin is a glucoside of salicylic alcohol, and oil of spiræa constitutes salicic aldehyd, while oil of wintergreen is composed largely of methylic salicate, as I have already explained. That some salicic grouping, moreover, occurs as a constituent residue of indigo C_8H_5NO, is shown by the following considerations. When, for example, indigo experiences decomposition by treatment with reagents, its single atom of nitrogen and one of its eight atoms of carbon are more particularly affected; and hence, as a convenient representation of its probable molecular constitution, we may associate this mobile carbon and nitrogen with one another, and so write the formula of indigo upon the 7-carbon or salicic type, thus:—

$C_7H_5(CN)O$.   Indigo or cyan-salicol

Now, by boiling indigo for a long time with oxidising agents, and by treating salicic acid with strong nitric acid, we obtain identically the same product, which has received the names of anilic, indigotic, and nitro-salicic acid, thus:—

Indigo		Oxygen		Anilic acid		Carb-anhyd.
$C_7H_5(CN)O$	+	O_6	=	$C_7H_5(NO_2)O_3$	+	CO_2
Salicic acid		Nitric acid		Nitro-salicic acid		Water
$C_7H_6O_3$	+	$(NO_2)HO$	=	$C_7H_5(NO_2)O_3$	+	$H.HO$

Again, when indigo is gently fused with caustic alkali it undergoes a simultaneous hydration and oxidation, whereby it is converted into anthranilic acid, thus:—

Indigo		Water		Oxygen		Anthranil. acid		Carb-anhyd.
$C_7H_5(CN)O$	+	H_2O	+	O_2	=	$C_7H_5(H_2N)O_2$	+	CO_2

When, however, the reaction takes place more violently, we get salicic acid produced instead, thus:—

Indigo		Water		Oxygen		Salicic acid		Carb-anhyd.		Ammonia
$C_7H_5(CN)O$	+	$2H_2O$	+	O_2	=	$C_7H_5(HO)O_2$	+	CO_2	+	H_3N

You observe that the anthranilic and salicic acids furnish us with another instance of that relationship between amidated and hydrated compounds to which I have so often adverted.

Seeing from the observations and researches of Prout, Heller, Debuyne, Hassall, Scheerer, Schunk, and others, that human urine not unfrequently deposits indigo spontaneously, and contains habitually an indigo-yielding substance known as indican, which is probably a glucoside of white or hydrogenised indigo, we come to the conclusion that while a salicic residue in the form of tyrosine is a constant product of the natural and artificial oxidation of nitrogenous tissue, another salicic residue in the form of indigo or indican is a usual ingredient of that secretion by which the products of disintegrated nitrogenous tissue are principally discharged. Moreover, this occurrence of indigo in urine further exemplifies a point with which we must all, I believe, have been more or less struck, both in this and previous lectures—namely, the thorough interdependence of vegetable and animal chemistry, as shown by the frequent relationship and even identity of products formed in vegetable and animal organisms.

(131.) Another physiological point of interest connected with salicic compounds is their occurrence in the urine in the form of salisuric acid. It is well known that when benzoic aldehyd or acid is taken internally, it makes its appearance in the urine in the form of glyco-benzoic or hippuric acid $C_9H_9NO_3$; and, no doubt, some, at any rate, of the hippuric acid excreted both by vegetable and mixed feeders is derived from the ingestion of certain benzo-genetic articles of food. Similarly, the administration of salicin and salicic aldehyd or acid is followed by the appearance in the urine of glyco-salicic or salisuric acid $C_9H_9NO_4$, readily decomposible into glycocine and salicic acid, just as hippuric acid is decomposible into glycocine and benzoic acid. Hence the salisuric and salicic acids may be regarded as normal constituents of the urine of the beaver, with which willow bark is well known to be a favourite food. The occurrence of salicic compounds in castoreum also is doubtless due in a similar manner to the food of the beaver. Castoreum, moreover, contains phenol, or coal-tar kreosote, which, according to Staedeler and others, is an ordinary constituent of human urine, and an important contributor to its characteristic odour. Now, the relation of phenol to salicic acid is very simple. Under suitable conditions salicic acid breaks up into phenol and carb-anhydride, which, under other conditions, re-unite to form salicic acid, thus:—

Phenol	Carb-anhyd.		Salicic acid
C_6H_6O	+ CO_2	=	$C_7H_6O_3$

Remembering that urine of a dark brown colour, or becoming of a brown colour by oxidation, contains a pigment which is in some way or other related to indigo, and also that an apparently similar brown urine is occasionally passed after the internal or external administration of phenol, kreosote, tar-oil, &c., this relationship of salicic and phenyl compounds presents a considerable pathological interest. Phenol may indeed be considered as the nucleus not only of salicic acid, but likewise of tyrosine and indigo; from both of which it is also readily obtainable. Moreover, by treatment with chlorine, all four bodies yield the same 6-carbon ultimate product, namely, chloranil $C_6Cl_4O_2$, or perchloroquinone.

(132.) It now only remains for us to consider the ultimate constitution of tyrosine, and its analogy to hippuric acid. Starting from water and ammonia, we have the following alcoholic derivatives:—

Hydrates

$\left.\begin{array}{l} H \\ H \end{array}\right\}$ O Hydric

$\left.\begin{array}{l} H \\ CH_3 \end{array}\right\}$ O Methylic

$\left.\begin{array}{l} H \\ C_2H_5 \end{array}\right\}$ O Ethylic

Amines

$\left.\begin{array}{l} H \\ H.H \end{array}\right\}$ N Hydr-amine

$\left.\begin{array}{l} H \\ CH_3.H \end{array}\right\}$ N Methyl-amine

$\left.\begin{array}{l} H \\ C_2H_5.H \end{array}\right\}$ N Ethyl-amine

Now, replacing an atom of hydrogen or the atom of chlorine, in acetic and chloracetic acid respectively, by the residue of water, HO, we obtain glycolic or oxiacetic acid; replacing it by the residue of ammonia, HHN, we obtain amid-acetic acid, or glycocine; replacing it by the residue of methylamine, CH_3HN, we obtain methyl-amid-acetic acid, or methyl-glycocine, or sarcosine; and, lastly, replacing it by the residue of ethylamine, C_2H_5HN, we obtain ethyl-amid-acetic acid, or ethyl-glycocine, thus:—

Acetic Derivatives

$C_2H_4O_2$ Acetic acid
$C_2H_3O_2(Cl)$ Chlor-acetic acid
$C_2H_3O_2(HO)$ Glycolic acid
$C_2H_3O_2(H_2N)$ Glycocine
$C_2H_3O_2(CH_4N)$ Sarcosine or methyl-glycocine .
$C_2H_3O_2(C_2H_6N)$ Ethyl-glycocine

The constitution and mutual relationship of the above tabulated bodies have been established as well by their recomposition as by their decomposition. In the case of tyrosine, however, we have only a knowledge of its decompositions to fall back upon, from which, however, it would appear, according to Schmitt and Nasse, that it corresponds most nearly in constitution with sarcosine or methyl-glycocine among natural products, and still more nearly with the artificial ethyl-glycocine of Heintz. Just, indeed, as sarcosine is acetic acid in which an atom of hydrogen is replaced by the residue of methylamine, so is tyrosine salicic acid in which an atom of hydrogen is replaced by the residue of ethylamine, thus:—

CONSTITUTION OF TYROSINE.   125

$C_2H_3(C H_3.HN)O_2$ Sarcosine, or methylamid-acetic acid
$C_7H_5(C_2H_5.HN)O_3$ Tyrosine, or ethylamid-salicic acid

(133.) Lastly, Dessaignes having prepared hippuric acid by substituting a residue of glycocine ($C_2H_3O_2$.HN) for the atom of chlorine in chlorobenzoic aldehyd C_7H_5(Cl)O, the relationship of hippuric acid and tyrosine to one another and to the benzoic and psrsalicic acids may be shown by the following formulæ, the parentheses of which are merely intended to point out the exchanged portions of the original and derived bodies:—

Benzoic acid	Hippuric acid
C_7H_5(HO)O	$C_7H_5(C_2H_3O_2.HN)O$
Persalicic acid	Tyrosine
$C_7H_5(HO)O_3$	$C_7H_5(C_2H_5.HN)O_3$

Now, ethylamine is indirectly convertible into glycocine by oxidation, whereas salicic acid is convertible into benzoic acid by deoxidation; or the fatty 2-carbon constituent of hippuric acid is more highly oxidised, whilst its aromatic 7-carbon constituent is less highly oxidised than are the corresponding residues of tyrosine.* Doubtless, therefore, the natural production of the two bodies by tissue metamorphosis takes place under different conditions. Their joint occurrence in the urine, however, together with that of indigo and phenol, confirms the inference we have already drawn—that be the chemical constitution of nitrogenous tissue what it may, there exist in its molecule one or more groupings belonging to the fatty family, and yielding fatty oxidation-products, together with one or more groupings belonging to the aromatic family, and yielding aromatic oxidation-products. In my next lecture we shall consider the intimate constitution of uric acid and its congeners.

* Since this lecture was delivered, Barth has rendered it probable that the aromatic constituent of tyrosine is not ordinary salicic acid, but the particular variety or isomer of it, which is known as paroxibenzoic acid.

LECTURE VI.

Uric acid—Its excretion throughout the animal kingdom—History of its chemical examination—Its undecomposibility save by oxidation—Probable pre-existence in it of urea—Classification of uric acid products into an-ureides, mon-ureides, and di-ureides—Also into carbonic, oxalic, and mesoxalic compounds—Oxidation of mesoxalic into oxalic, and of oxalic into carbonic acid—Ureides formed by an elimination of either one or two atoms of water—Hydrogenised carbonic, oxalic, and mesoxalic compounds—Table of uric acid products—Additional intermediate and amidated bodies—Oxalic mon-ureides and di-ureides—Mesoxalic mon-ureides associated with barbituric acid—Mesoxalic di-ureides, including hypoxanthine, xanthine, and uric acid—Their mutual convertibility—Relationship of xanthine to guanine The pseudo-uric and uroxanic acids—Uric acid viewed simply as a compound of carbonic oxide and urea—Excretion of urate of ammonia by birds and insects—Dynamic values of oxidation into uric acid and urea respectively—Function of lungs supplemented by discharge of uric acid from kidneys—Tissue metamorphosis affected by alterative medicines—Activity of loosely combined oxygen—Nitric oxide as a carrier of active oxygen—Comparison of iodine with nitric peroxide—Resemblances and differences between iodine and chlorine—Their action as oxygenants in presence of water—Free chlorine more active than iodine, and combined iodine more mobile than chlorine—Reducing action of iodhydric acid—Alterative action of iodine dependent on its chemical mobility—Similar characters of arsenic, mercury, &c.—Effect of alkalies on tissue-oxidation—Gorup-Besanez's experiments with ozone—Conclusion.

(134.) OF all the incompletely oxidised products of tissue-metamorphosis, uric acid is, I suppose, the most important, whether regarded from a physiological and pathological, or from a purely chemical point of view. In combination, chiefly with ammonia, it forms the principal urinary constituent voided by insects, land-reptiles, and birds. Normally, it occurs but in small proportion in the urine of man, while it is found in yet smaller proportion in that of carnivorous, and can scarcely be said to exist—if, indeed, it does habitually exist—in that of herbivorous and omnivorous quadrupeds. According to various authorities, it is to be found constantly in the juices of the human spleen, liver, lungs, and brain. The merest traces of it are also met with normally in blood, but its proportion therein under particular forms of disease, such as albuminuria, and more especially gout, becomes very appreciable. In certain cases of gout, indeed, all the fluids of the body are found more or less saturated with uric acid, and some of them even supersaturated, so as to deposit those well-known concretions of urate of sodium, commonly called chalkstones. I need scarcely refer also to the frequent excess of uric acid discharged by the human kidneys, under greater or less derangements of bodily health, and to its deposition in the forms of urinary sediment, gravel, and calculus. Now this acid, as shown by its formula $C_5N_4H_4O_3$, consists of only sixteen elementary atoms, and is consequently, as regards its ultimate composition, a far more simple body than many of those we have previously considered. Nevertheless, the problem of its intimate constitution for a long time baffled all attempts at solution, and cannot, even at the present day, be considered as quite satisfactorily unravelled.

(135.) Uric acid was discovered in 1776 by the renowned Swedish chemist, Scheele; but it was first submitted to a minute investigation by Liebig and Wöhler, whose efforts resulted in the production and identification, among other new bodies, of alloxantine, alloxanic acid, dialuric acid, uramile, mesoxalic acid, allantoine, mycomelic acid, parabanic acid, &c., and whose admirable work, published in 1838, forms the broad and sound basis of all our subsequent knowledge. These chemists had been preceded by Brugnatelli and Prout—the discoverers of alloxan and murexide respectively—and were succeeded more particularly by Schlieper, Pelouze, Fritzsche, Gregory, and Hlasiwetz. To the number of bodies already described, Schlieper added the leucoturic, allituric, dilituric, hydantoic, hydurilic, and allanturic or lantanuric acids— the last also discovered by Pelouze. In 1853, Gerhardt, in his celebrated 'Traité de Chimie Organique,' gave a very complete account of the then known uric acid products, and, by dividing them into two well-defined natural groups, simplified very greatly the conception of their origins and metamorphoses. Among subsequent workers, Strecker has added considerably to our knowledge; and Baeyer has increased the list of compounds by his discovery of pseudo-uric acid, hydantoine, violantine, and the violuric and barbituric acids, the last-named being a body of very great interest; while he has also thrown considerable light upon the nature of the bodies previously discovered by Schlieper. Moreover, adopting Gerhardt's classification as a basis, and viewing both old and new products from the extreme height of modern doctrine, he has published by far the most complete and connected account of the uric acid group of compounds which has hitherto been given to the world. The scheme which I am about to bring under your notice, and which, I think I may say, is even more comprehensive, does not differ greatly from that of Baeyer in principle, and is indebted very largely to him for its elaboration. I propose, however, to differ from him in disregarding altogether the molecular arrangement of the different compounds, preferring to limit myself in this, as in previous lectures, simply to questions of origin and relationship.

(136.) I have already told you that the great majority of complex organic bodies are built up of the residues of comparatively simple molecules; that hippuric acid, for instance, is constituted of the residues of benzoic acid and glycocine, while tyrosine is constituted of the residues of salicic acid and ethylamine—the glycocine and ethylamine themselves containing residues of ammonia and of glycolic acid and alcohol respectively. Now, uric acid is evidently built up in a similar manner, and contains the residues of several constituent molecules. But a hitherto insuperable difficulty in determining its exact mode of construction arises from the circumstance of its never having been decomposed into the actual molecules of which its constituent residues are the representatives, but only into the oxidised, or rather dehydrogenised, products of these molecules. Add to uric acid an atom of oxygen, so as to burn off two of its atoms of hydrogen, and it breaks up with the greatest ease, though without this additional oxygen it has hitherto proved undecomposible. You will observe from its formula, $C_5N_4H_4O_3$, that uric acid contains five atoms of carbon and four atoms of nitrogen, while urea CN_2H_4O, contains only one atom of carbon and two atoms of nitrogen. Accordingly, we find that when dehydrogenised uric acid undergoes complete decomposition by an absorption of water, it breaks up into two molecules of urea (containing C_2N_4) and one molecule of a non-nitrogenous 3-carbon acid. Whether, however, the residues of the two molecules of urea, obtainable by the oxidation or dehydrogenation of uric acid, pre-exist in uric acid, the 3-carbon acid alone being the dehydrogenised product, or whether the residue of the resulting 3-carbon acid pre-exists in uric acid, the two atoms of urea being formed by dehydrogenation, there is no evidence to show. The great stability of uric acid under treatment with even strong acids and alkalies is certainly opposed to its containing pre-formed residues of urea, since in all undoubtedly so constituted bodies the residues of urea are removable or decomposible with the greatest facility. On the other hand, the assumption of pre-existent urea-residues in uric acid very greatly facilitates our conception of its decompositions, and, receiving the general consent of chemists, may, I think, be provisionally admitted by us on the present occasion.

(137.) Be this as it may, when uric acid is subjected to an oxidising agent in presence of water, it gives up two of its atoms of hydrogen to the oxidising agent, while the dehydrogenised product reacts with water to form mesoxalic acid and urea. Employing chlorine as the oxidising agent, we have the following reaction,—

Chlorine	Uric acid	Water	Mesoxalic	Urea	Chlorhydric
Cl_2 +	$C_5N_4H_4O_3$ +	$4H_2O$ =	$C_3H_4O_5$ +	$2CN_2H_4O$ +	$2HCl$;

or, supposing the reaction with water to take place after the removal of the hydrogen by chlorine,—

K

Dehyd-uric?		Water		Mesoxalic		Urea
$C_5N_4H_2O_3$	+	$4H_2O$	=	$C_3H_2O_5$	+	$2CN_2H_4O.$

In the above equations I have represented both atoms of urea to be simultaneously separated from the mesoxalic acid; but in reality their separation is usually effected at two successive stages, the first of which results in the formation of alloxan, and the second in its decomposition, thus:—

Dehyd-uric?		Water		Alloxan		Urea
$C_5N_4H_2O_3$	+	$2H_2O$	=	$C_4N_2H_2O_4$	+	$CN_2H_4O.$
Alloxan		Water		Mesoxalic		Urea
$C_4N_2H_2O_4$	+	$2H_2O$	=	$C_3H_2O_5$	+	$CN_2H_4O.$

We have, you perceive, three mesoxalic compounds, first the non-nitrogenous acid, then the compound of the acid with one atom of urea minus $2H_2O$, and lastly, the compound of the acid with two atoms of urea minus $4H_2O$, thus:—

Mesoxalic	Alloxan	Dehyd-uric?
$C_3H_2O_5$	$C_4N_2H_2O_4$	$C_5N_4H_2O_3$

Now, by hydrogenising mesoxalic acid, we obtain **tartronic acid** $C_3H_4O_5$, and by hydrogenising alloxan we obtain **dialuric acid** $C_4N_2H_4O_4$, which two bodies accordingly bear to uric acid the same relation that mesoxalic acid and alloxan bear to dehyd-uric acid, thus,—

Tartronic	Dialuric	Uric acid
$C_3H_4O_5$	$C_4N_2H_4O_4$	$C_5N_4H_4O_3;$

and, just as our hypothetical dehyd-uric acid yields mesoxalic acid and alloxan, so should actual uric acid yield us the tartronic and dialuric acids.

In reality, however, these bodies have not been obtained by the mere breaking up of uric acid, but only by rehydrogenising the mesoxalic acid and alloxan which result from the breaking up of its dehydrogenised product. Despite, however, this flaw in the demonstration, we may provisionally, as I have said, regard the dialuric and uric acids as tartron-ureide and tartron-diureide respectively.

(138.) The several bodies I have just mentioned are typical of three well-defined classes of compounds, to one or other of which the immense number of uric acid products are, with but very few exceptions, assignable. We have first the class of simple non-nitrogenous acids, or an-ureides, like the tartronic and mesoxalic acids. Then we have the class of bodies containing a residue of the acid plus one residue of urea, or the mon-ureides, such as dialuric acid and alloxan; and lastly, we have the class of bodies containing a residue of the acid plus two residues of urea, or the di-ureides, such as uric acid itself. Confining our present attention to the an-ureides, let us consider briefly their derivation and mutual relationship. Mesoxalic acid, then, the most complex non-nitrogenous product obtainable directly from uric acid, constitutes the third term in the following series:—

An-ureides

CH_2O_3	Carbonic.
$C_2H_2O_4$	Oxalic.
$C_3H_2O_5$	Mesoxalic.

Oxalic acid, you observe, differs in composition from carbonic acid by one atom of carbonic oxide CO, in excess; while mesoxalic acid differs in composition from oxalic acid by a further atom of carbonic oxide CO, in excess. Now, when mesoxalic acid is acted upon by nascent oxygen O, its excess of carbonic oxide CO, is removed in the form of carb-anhydride CO_2, so as to leave oxalic acid, thus;—

Mesoxalic	Oxygen		Carb-anhyd.		Oxalic
$C_3H_2O_5$	+ O	=	CO_2	+	$C_2H_2O_4$.

Hence when uric acid is subjected to a more active oxidation than suffices to produce mesoxalic acid we obtain oxalic acid, which may occur in its simple an-ureide state, or conjugated with one atom of urea to form a mon-ureide such as parabanic acid, or conjugated with two atoms of urea to form a diureide, such as mycomelic acid, a body having exactly the same relation to oxalic acid that uric has to mesoxalic acid.

(139.) Now, just as we can convert mesoxalic into oxalic acid by burning off its excess of carbonic oxide, so may we convert oxalic acid itself into carbonic acid by a precisely similar oxidation, thus:—

$$\underset{\text{Oxalic}}{C_2H_2O_4} + \underset{\text{Oxygen}}{O} = \underset{\text{Carb-anhyd.}}{CO_2} + \underset{\text{Carbonic}}{CH_2O_3}.$$

The rapidity with which the oxidation of oxalic acid can be effected is easily capable of experimental illustration. In this tall beaker, for instance, I place some ordinary black oxide or peroxide of manganese MnO_2, a compound which readily parts with one of its two atoms of oxygen to become converted into protoxide of manganese MnO; while I introduce into the flask an ounce or so of commercial oxalic acid. Now, upon drenching the acid with hot water and pouring the resulting mixture of solution and crystals upon the oxide of manganese, we get, you perceive, a most rapid oxidation of the oxalic acid, accompanied by a violent effervescence of carb-anhydride gas which we shall be able to recognise in a minute or two by its high specific gravity and by its power of extinguishing flame and rendering lime-water turbid. The effervescence is at first so great as to be almost unmanageable, and a very slight agitation would cause the liquid contents to froth over the beaker; but now that the action is a little moderated I may prove to you the nature of the gas evolved by pouring some of it on to a lighted taper, which you see is immediately extinguished; and by pouring some more of it upon this clear solution of lime, which by agitation therewith is immediately converted into an opaque mixture of chalk and water. Hence, when uric acid is subjected to a more powerful oxidation than suffices to produce oxalic acid, we obtain carbonic acid, which, like the oxalic and mesoxalic acids, is also capable of colligation with urea. No ureide of carbonic acid, indeed, has yet been formed directly from uric acid—the active treatment required to effect the complete oxidation of the uric acid effecting also a separation from one another of the resulting carbonic acid and urea, which, however, may be obtained in combination by other means. Allophanic acid, for instance, is a well known artificial mon-ureide of carbonic acid, but so far as I am aware no di-ureide of the acid has hitherto been produced by any process whatsoever.

(140.) The mon-ureide of mesoxalic acid, of which I have already spoken—namely, alloxan, is formed from mesoxalate of urea by an elimination of two atoms of water ; but there is another ureide—namely, alloxanic acid, which differs from the original salt by the loss of only one atom of water. Similarly oxalic acid forms two mon-ureides—namely, parabanic acid or paraban analogous to alloxan, and oxaluric analogous to alloxanic acid. Carbonic acid, however, forms but a single ureide, which is produced by the elimination of only one atom of water, and accordingly belongs to the same series as the oxaluric and alloxanic acids, thus : —

Acids		Ureides	
CH_2O_3	Carbonic	$C_2N_2H_4O_3$	Allophanic.
		— —	„
$C_2H_2O_4$	Oxalic	$C_3N_2H_4O_4$	Oxaluric.
		$C_3N_2H_2O_3$	Paraban.
$C_3H_2O_5$	Mesoxalic	$C_4N_2H_4O_5$	Alloxanic.
		$C_4N_2H_2O_4$	Alloxan.

Similarly among the di-ureides, some are formed from their corresponding mon-ureides by an elimination of one atom, and others by an elimination of two atoms of water.

(141.) Now, mesoxalic acid is convertible by deoxidation or hydrogenation into tartronic acid, as I have already observed; and by pushing the deoxidation a stage further we obtain malonic acid, both of them capable of forming mon-ureides and di-ureides; and, in a similar manner, the oxalic and carbonic acids furnish a variety of similarly behaving deoxidation-products. When we consider, then, the total number of carbonic or 1-carbon, of oxalic or 2-carbon, and of mesoxalic or 3-carbon, hydrogenised products; and that the majority of these products, like their original acids, are capable of forming mon-ureides by an elimination of one atom, and other mon-ureides by an elimination of two atoms of water; and, further, that many of these mon-ureides are capable of forming di-ureides by a further elimination of one atom, and other di-ureides by a further elimination of two atoms of water, we are no longer surprised at the great number and variety of known compounds belonging to the uric acid group, and shall not be surprised at the discovery of very many more. The most important of those already known are included in the following table. It is divided perpendicularly into three columns of an-ureides, mon-ureides, and di-ureides; and horizontally into three layers of carbonic, oxalic, and mesoxalic products. The compounds connected by means of dotted lines differ in composition from one another by an excess or deficit of one atom of urea minus one atom of water; while those standing on the same level in the adjoining columns and unconnected by dotted lines, differ from one another by an excess or deficit of one atom of urea minus two atoms of water.

An-ureides		Mon-ureides		Di-ureides	
CH_4O	Methylic	$C_2N_2H_6O$	Methyl-urea		
CH_2O_3	Carbonic	$C_2N_2H_4O_3$	Allophanic		
		$C_3N_2H_6O_2$	Acet-urea	— —	,,
		$C_3N_2H_6O_3$	Hydantoic	$C_4N_4H_6O_2$	Glycoluril
		— —	,,	$C_4N_4H_6O_3$	Allantoine
$C_2H_4O_2$	Acetic				
$C_2H_4O_3$	Glycolic	$C_3N_2H_4O_2$	Hydantoine	— —	,,
$C_2H_4O_4$	Glyoxylic	$C_3N_2H_4O_3$	Lantanuric	$C_4N_4H_4O_2$	Mycomelic
		$C_3N_2H_4O_4$	Oxaluric	— —	,,
$C_2H_2O_3$	Glyoxalic				
$C_2H_2O_4$	Oxalic	$C_3N_2H_2O_3$	Parabanic	— —	,,
— —	,,	— —	,,	$C_5N_4H_4O$	Hypoxanth.
$C_3H_4O_4$	Malonic	$C_4N_2H_4O_3$	Barbituric	$C_5N_4H_4O_2$	Xanthine
$C_3H_4O_5$	Tartronic	$C_4N_2H_4O_4$	Dialuric	$C_5N_4H_4O_3$	Uric acid
— —	,,	$C_4N_2H_4O_5$	Alloxanic	$C_5N_4H_6O_4$	Pseudo-uric
$C_3H_2O_5$	Mesoxalic	$C_4N_2H_2O_4$	Alloxan	— —	,,

(142.) Even this table, however, is far from being complete. Thus I have introduced only one alcoholic urea as a type—namely, the methylic, excluding its homologues. I have also omitted uroxanic acid and several amidated and nitro-compounds, to which I shall presently refer. Moreover, between some of the consecutive mon-ureides shown in the table, there exist diameric bodies formed by the union of the two consecutive mon-ureides with elimination of water. Allituric acid, for instance, is a diamerone of hydantoine and lantanuric acid; while leucoturic acid is a diamerone of lantanuric acid and oxaluric or parabanic acid, thus:—

Allituric		Water		Hydantoine		Lantanuric
$C_6N_4H_6O_4$	+	H_2O	=	$C_3N_2H_4O_2$	+	$C_3N_2H_4O_3$.
Leucoturic		Water		Lantanuric		Parabanic
$C_6N_4H_4O_5$	+	H_2O	=	$C_3N_2H_4O_3$	+	$C_3N_2H_2O_3$.

In a precisely similar manner, among mesoxalic compounds we have hydurilic acid, a diamerone of barbituric acid and dialuric acid; while alloxantine is a diamerone of dialuric acid and alloxanic acid or alloxan, thus:—

Hydurilic		Water		Barbituric		Dialuric
$C_8N_4H_6O_6$	+	H_2O	=	$C_4N_2H_4O_3$	+	$C_4N_2H_4O_4$.
Alloxantine		Water		Dialuric		Alloxan
$C_8N_4H_4O_7$	+	H_2O	=	$C_4N_2H_4O_4$	+	$C_4N_2H_2O_4$.

(143.) Of the many bodies above formulated, only a few call for any special remark. Hydantoic acid is also known as glycoluric acid, which is, perhaps, a better name for it. Again, the body here called lantanuric acid is probably identical with the allanturic acid of Pelouze, and also with difluan. Oxaluric acid is interesting from the alleged occurrence of its calcium-salt in human urine, in the form of the dumb-bell crystals so often associated with octahedral crystals of the oxalate. That these dumb-bells may consist of oxalurate of calcium, as suggested by their discoverer, Golding Bird, is not indeed improbable; but the evidence that they really are so constituted is anything but satisfactory. The relations of lantanuric and oxaluric acids to another uric acid product known as oxaluramide are obviously those of hydrogen and water to ammonia, as illustrated in the case of so many previously considered compounds, thus:—

H.H	Hydrogen	$C_3N_2H_3(H)O_3$	Lantanuric.
H.HO	Water	$C_3N_2H_3(HO)O_3$	Oxaluric.
H.H$_2$N	Ammonia	$C_3N_2H_3(H_2N)O_3$	Oxaluramide.

Allantoine, as shown by the fine specimen lent me by Messrs. Hopkins and Williams, is a beautiful crystalline body existing in the allantoic fluid of the fœtal, and in the urine of the sucking calf. It has also been noticed by Frerichs and Städeler in the urine of two dogs, upon whose lungs they had been experimenting, and is easily procurable from uric acid by oxidation with peroxide of lead. By deoxidation, it yields glycoluril (Rheineck).

Mycomelic acid may be obtained, among other processes, by heating uric acid with water under pressure,* thus:—

Uric acid		Mycomelic acid		Carbonic oxide
$C_5N_4H_4O_3$	=	$C_4N_4H_4O_2$	+	CO.

As I have before observed, it stands to paraban in exactly the same relation that uric acid stands to alloxan. From the observations of Hlasiwetz it seems probable that some supposed urate of ammonia deposits, occurring in urine, really consist of mycomelic acid, which similarly evolves ammonia when treated with alkalies, and yields murexide when evaporated with nitric acid.

(144.) Of mesoxalic mon-ureides, alloxan and barbituric acid appear to be the most important. Alloxan, the first discovered product of the artificial oxidation of uric acid, has recently been recognised by Liebig as a pre-formed constituent of urine. By treatment with bromine, it yields dibromobarbituric acid,

* Possibly, thus:—

Uric acid		Water		Mycomelic		Formic
$C_5N_4H_4O_3$	+	H_2O	=	$C_4N_4H_4O_2$	+	CH_2O_2.

convertible by successive hydrogenation into bromobarbituric, and barbituric acid, which last serves as a sort of nucleus in the following series of compounds :—

Mesoxalic Mon-ureides

$C_4N_2H_2(HO)_2O_3$	Alloxanic.
$C_4N_2H_2(Br_2)O_3$	Dibromobarbituric,
$C_4N_2H_4O_3$	Barbituric.
$C_4N_2H_3(Br)O_3$	Bromobarbituric.
$C_4N_2H_3(HO)O_3$	Dialuric.
$C_4N_2H_3(H_2N)O_3$	Uramile.
$C_4N_2H_3(H_2NSO_3)O_3$	Thionuric.
$C_4N_2H_3(NO)O_3$	Violuric.
$C_4N_2H_3(NO_2)O_3$	Dilituric.
$C_8N_4H_6(N_2O_3)O_6$	Violantine.

The last body on the list—namely, violantine—seems to be not a diamerone or residuary, but a completed compound of the violuric and dilituric acids. It is observable that the mutual relationship of barbituric acid, dialuric acid, and uramile in this sub-group is strictly parallel to that of lantanuric acid, oxaluric acid, and oxaluramide in the preceding one. Moreover, the malonic and barbituric acids are homologous with the oxalic and parabanic acids respectively; or, in other words, the most oxidised of known 2-carbon uric acid products are homologically the representatives of the least oxidised 3-carbon products thus,—

$C_2H_2O_4$	Oxalic	$C_3N_2H_2O_3$	Parabanic
$C_3H_4O_4$	Malonic	$C_4N_2H_4O_3$	Barbituric;

although from another point of view they correspond more nearly with mesoxalic acid and alloxan, as I have already remarked.

(145.) The relationship subsisting between the three mesoxaldi-ureides, though long suspected from the similarity of their formulæ—hypoxanthine $C_5N_4H_4O$, xanthine $C_5N_4H_4O_2$, and uric acid $C_5N_4H_4O_3$—has but very recently received an experimental demonstration at the hands of Strecker and Rheineck. With the first of these bodies, or hypoxanthine, originally found by Scheerer in human and bovine splenic juices, the so-called sarcine, subsequently discovered by Strecker in juice of flesh, and thought to be a distinct base, has since proved to be identical. From the results of Scheerer, Strecker, Gorup-Besanez, and others, it appears that hypoxanthine exists to a very appreciable extent in most glandular juices and in muscular tissue, particularly of the heart, while it has also been recognised in brain-substance and in the blood and urine. It occurs as a white crystalline powder, insoluble in cold and sparingly soluble in hot water. Strecker has shown that by oxidation with nitric acid, it yields xanthine, and gives accordingly with nitric acid, the characteristic reaction of xanthine—a compound which has also been detected in blood and in most animal juices. Under the name of xanthic oxide, it was discovered in 1819 by the elder Marcet, in a variety of urinary calculus which subsequent experience has proved to be very rare. It has been met with, more frequently indeed, though still very seldom, as an amorphous urinary deposit, and in one case recorded by Bence Jones it occurred in lozenge-shaped crystals. Its habitual presence, however, in small quantity, as a dissolved constituent of urine, seems now to be very well established. Xanthine, moreover, is not only known as a urinary, but also as an intestinal concretion, for Göbel has met with it as the chief constituent of certain oriental bezoar stones obtained from ruminating animals. I have already mentioned Strecker's artificial production of xanthine by the oxidation of hypoxanthine or sarcine with nitric acid. Conversely, Strecker and Rheineck have very recently shown that uric acid, by deoxidation with sodium-amalgam, yields a mixture of xanthine and hypoxanthine, the latter in greatest proportion, so that the actual relationship of the three bodies is now placed beyond all question. Hitherto hypoxanthine and xanthine, having been obtained in small quantities only, have not been subjected to any detailed examination. It can scarcely be doubted, however, that xanthine is a mon-ureide of barbituric and a di-ureide of malonic acid, in the same sense that uric acid is a mon-ureide of dialuric and a di-ureide of tartronic acid. We may hope, indeed, to have these relations very soon established by experiment; for, even if it should not prove possible to prepare xanthine advantageously from uric acid, still the fact of its close relationship therewith would lead us to expect its more abundant existence than has hitherto been imagined—particularly, for instance, in the excreta of those animals whose normal mode of tissue-waste results in the production of uric acid rather than of urea.

(146.) This expectation is strengthened by the extraction from guano, the well-known dried excrement of sea-fowl, of a feeble base called guanine, which bears to xanthine the same often-referred-to relation that ammonia bears to water, as shown in the following series of formulæ :—

$C_5N_4H_3(H)O$ Hypoxanthine.
$C_5N_4H_3(HO)O$ Xanthine.
$C_5N_4H_3(H_2N)O$ Guanine.
$C_5N_4H_2(HO)_2O$ Uric acid.

Just, in fact, as uric acid, and doubtless xanthine, yield by oxidation parabanic acid and urea, so does guanine yield by oxidation parabanic acid and amido-urea or guanidine,* thus:—

Xanthine   Parabanic   Urea
$C_5N_4H_3(HO)O + H_2O + O_3 = C_3N_2H_2O_3 + CN_2H_3(HO) + CO_2?$

Guanine   Parabanic   Guanidine
$C_5N_4H_3(H_2N)O + H_2O + O_3 = C_3N_2H_2O_3 + CN_2H_3(H_2N) + CO_2.$

Moreover, xanthine itself occurs in small quantity as a secondary product of the above oxidation of guanine, and may be obtained

---

* By the oxidation of kreatine, which has been already described as a polymerone of glycolic acid, methylamine, and urea, its glycolic residue is converted into oxalic acid, while its methylamine and urea residues are left in combination to form methylamido-urea or methyluramine, a compound homologous with amido-urea or guanidine, thus:—

   $CN_2H_3(HO)$ Urea.
   $CN_2H_3(H_2N)$ Guanidine.
   $CN_2H_3(CH_3HN)$ Methyluramine.

Again, biuret $C_2N_3H_5O_2$, or $C_2N_2H_3(H_2N)O_2$, may be regarded as carboguanidinic acid, just as allophan $C_2N_2H_4O_3$ or $C_2N_2H_3(HO)O_2$ is regarded as carb-ureic acid.

in larger quantity by treating guanine with nitrous acid, according to the general method adopted for converting amidated into hydrated bodies, thus:—

Guanine   Nitrous   Xanthine

$$C_5N_4H_3(H_2N)O + (HO)NO = C_5N_4H_3(HO)O + N_2 + H_2O.$$

That the guanine extracted from guano is a constituent of the birds' excrement as voided, and not a product of decomposition, is rendered probable by its occurrence under other circumstances. Thus it forms the chief portion of the excrement of the garden spider, has been recognised by Scheerer in the pancreas of the horse, and is occasionally met with in human urine.

(147.) We have now only left for consideration the pseudo-uric and uroxanic acids, which we may regard as terms in the following series:—

$$\begin{array}{lllll}
& & & C_5N_4H_4 \ O_3 & \text{Uric.} \\
C_5N_4H_4O_3 & + & H_2O & = C_5N_4H_6 \ O_4 & \text{Pseudo-uric.} \\
C_5N_4H_4O_3 & + & 2H_2O & = C_5N_4H_8 \ O_5 & \text{,,} \\
C_5N_4H_4O_3 & + & 3H_2O & = C_5N_4H_{10}O_6 & \text{Uroxanic.} \\
C_5N_4H_4O_3 & + & 4H_2O & = C_3H_4O_5 & \text{Tartronic} + 2CN_2H_4O \text{ Urea?}
\end{array}$$

Pseudo-uric acid is a recent discovery of Baeyer's. It has not actually been produced by the direct or indirect hydration of uric acid, but only by the combination of cyanic acid vapour with uramile or amido-barbituric acid. Just, in fact, as cyanic acid converts ammonia into anomalous cyanate of ammonia or urea, so does it convert the residue of ammonia contained in uramile into a residue of urea, thereby changing the amido-monureide into a simple diureide, thus:—

Uramile   Cyanic acid   Pseudo-uric

$$C_4N_2H_3(NH_2)O_3 + CNHO = C_4N_2H_3(CN_2H_3O)O_3 \text{ or } C_5N_4H_6O_4.$$

Pseudo-uric acid occurs as a white crystalline almost insoluble powder. Hitherto it has not proved dehydrateable into uric acid; but by dehydrogenation, in presence of water, it behaves like uric acid, breaking up into alloxan and urea. The compound $C_5N_4H_8O_5$ is unknown, while uroxanic acid $C_5N_4H_{10}O_6$, is known but very imperfectly. Unlike pseudo-uric acid, it really results from the absorption of water by uric acid, and is produced in the form of its potassium-salt by boiling uric acid for a long time in solution of caustic potash. In the free state it occurs as a white, glistening, sparingly soluble powder. The absorption of a fourth atom of water by uric acid would doubtless lead, not to the formation of a new hydrate, but to the breaking up of the acid itself, most likely into tartronic acid and urea.

(148.) I have already referred to upwards of forty uric acid products, by no means all that are known, and I have indicated the existence of many more, as yet unknown, to fill up gaps in the different series. Now, when we reflect that in all probability most of these compounds, actual and problematical, do not stand alone, but are associated each with a more or less numerous set of isomers,—that is to say, of bodies having the same ultimate composition, but a different molecular arrangement—we scarcely venture to contemplate the almost overwhelming intricacy with which we are threatened. To us, as physicians, however, the subject is capable of assuming a simpler aspect. On any view of its constitution, hydrated uric acid differs in composition from two atoms of urea by the addition of three atoms of carbonic oxide CO, capable of oxidation into carb-anhydride CO_2, and by that oxidation of generating a certain amount of heat, or its equivalent of motion :—

Water	Uric acid	Oxygen	Carb-anhyd.	Urea
$2H_2O$ +	$C_5N_4H_4O_3$ +	O_3		
or	$C_3O_3(CN_2H_4O)_2$ +	O_3	= $3CO_2$ +	$2CN_2H_4O$.

Hence, uric acid must be considered to result from an incomplete oxidation of nitrogenous tissue, whereby, in addition to urea, carbonic oxide is produced instead of carbonic anhydride. In accordance with this deduction, then, we are not surprised to find that the tissue-metamorphosis of reptiles, whose motions are so sluggish and temperature is so low, should yield imperfectly burned and used carbonic oxide in the form of uric acid, or rather urate of ammonia, instead of the perfectly burnt and used carb-anhydride excreted by mammals. On the other hand, this view seems at first sight altogether discordant with the similar excretion of urate of ammonia by birds and insects, whose motions are so active and temperatures so high. But by having regard to the following considerations, it will, I think, appear that the loss, or rather non-liberation, of force resulting from the merely half-burning, so to speak, of the excess of carbon excreted as uric acid, is less than at first sight appears, and is, moreover, largely compensated for by certain consequent advantages.

(149.) For reasons which I cannot now discuss, the experimental results actually obtained on the quantities of heat evolved by the combustion of carbon into carbonic oxide and anhydride respectively, are not applicable to the point we have under our consideration, which at present therefore can only be decided from analogy and general principles. Let us then imagine the production of carbonic oxide and anhydride under conditions as nearly as possible analogous. Let us conceive, for instance, that an atom of carbon first unites with an atom of oxygen gas to form solid carbonic oxide CO, which then unites with a second atom of oxygen gas to form solid carb-anhydride CO_2. Remembering, as explained in my fourth lecture, that the heat produced by any combination is the exact measure of the force required to separate the constituents of the compound from one another, and is, indeed, only a setting free of the heat which at some time or other was absorbed in the act of their separation, it will follow, provided the two atoms of oxygen in carb-anhydride are retained by the carbon with an equally strong affinity, that the amount of heat evolved by the combustion of carbon into solid carbonic oxide will be just one half of that evolved by its combustion into solid carb-anhydride. But we have good reason for believing that the first atom of oxygen in carb-anhydride is more firmly retained than the second atom, and consequently that the amount of heat liberated by the combination of the first atom is greater than that liberated by the combination of the second atom of oxygen; or, in other words, that the heat evolved in the production of solid carbonic oxide CO, is more than half of that evolved in the production of solid carb-anhydride CO_2.

(150.) But we are actually concerned with a comparison of the amounts of heat evolved in the oxidation of tissue-carbon into the solid carbonic oxide constituent of uric acid on the one hand, and into the gaseous carb-anhydride discharged from the lungs on the other. Now it would appear that the latent heat of gaseous carbon, or the quantity of heat absorbed in its vaporisation, amounts to fully $\frac{1}{3}$ of that evolved by its mere combustion into carb-anhydride;* so that the ratio of the heat evolved by the combustion of carbon into gaseous carb-anhydride CO_2, to the heat evolved by its combustion into solid carbonic oxide CO, would be as $\frac{2}{3}$ to $\frac{1}{2}$ (more exactly as $\frac{96}{136}$ to $\frac{68}{136}$), or of course as 1 to $\frac{3}{4}$ —even leaving out of consideration the probable excess of heat developed in the production of solid carbonic oxide over that developed in its conversion into solid carb-anhydride. By the discharge, then, of uric acid, instead of carb-anhydride and urea, there is a loss of 50 per cent. of heat by imperfect oxidation, minus a gain of 25 per cent. of heat by the discharge from the body of solid carbon and oxygen in the form of uric acid, instead of gaseous carbon and oxygen in the form of carb-anhydride.

I am aware that in arriving at this conclusion, which is avowedly based on assumption, several modifying actions of more or less importance have been disregarded; still I think it cannot be doubted that the amount of heat produced by the conversion of tissue-carbon into the carbonic oxide constituent of uric acid is more nearly $\frac{1}{4}$ than $\frac{1}{2}$ of that produced by its conversion into gaseous carb-anhydride. Moreover, the amount of oxygen consumed in the production of carbonic oxide being only one-half of that consumed in the production of carb-anhydride, the amount

* While 12+16 grammes of carbonic oxide CO, in uniting with 16 grammes of oxygen O, evolve 68 units of heat, 12 grammes of carbon C, in uniting with twice 16 grammes of oxygen O_2, evolve not 136, but only 96 units of heat; the difference between 136 and 96, or 40 units of heat, being absorbed in changing the 16 grammes of carbon from the solid to the gaseous state. This calculation leaves out of consideration the heat absorbed and evolved respectively, in the conversion of one volume of oxygen into two volumes of carbonic oxide, and of two volumes of carbonic oxide plus one volume of oxygen into two volumes of carb-anhydride.

of cold air necessary to be inspired and heated up to the temperature of the animal will be only half as much in the one case as in the other, whereby a further economy of heat will be effected.

(151.) But in the liberation of pent-up force within the body, we have to consider not only the tissue burnt, but also the oxygen required to burn it. Now it is quite conceivable that in the organism of birds, for instance, an economy of oxygen or breath may be of more importance than an economy of tissue or food.* Indeed, the marvellous adoption in predatory birds of every supplemental contrivance for increasing ever so slightly their respiratory surface, without, however, departing from its almost reptilian type of structure, is strongly suggestive of these animals being, so to speak, under-lunged, and of the necessity for economising their lung-action in every possible way. Now admitting the correctness of our former conclusion, that by the transformation of a given amount of tissue-carbon into the carbonic oxide constituent of uric acid, there is liberated say $\frac{1}{4}$ of the actual energy produceable by its oxidation into gaseous carb-anhydride, it follows conversely that the transformation of two atoms of oxygen into the carbonic oxide constituent of uric acid C_2O_2, will liberate $1\frac{1}{2}$ times the actual energy producible by its transformation into carb-anhydride CO_2. So that while for a given amount of tissue-carbon we obtain 25 per cent. less, for a given amount of oxygen we obtain 50 per cent. more heat by the production of the carbonic oxide constituent of uric acid, than by the production of gaseous carb-anhydride; or an atom of oxygen is employed with 50 per cent. more economy in the one case than in the other.

(152.) Moreover, the lungs, it must be remembered, act not only as receivers of oxygen but also as dischargers of carbon from

---

* 'Of all animals birds are most dependent upon a constant renewal of the air in their lungs, and upon the purity of that with which they are supplied. Most birds will die in air which has been but slightly charged with carbonic acid, and which can be respired by mammals without immediate injury.'—Carpenter's 'Principles of Physiology, General and Comparative,' 3rd ed. p. 758.

the body, and, in this particular, we find the lungs of birds materially aided by the ejection from their kidneys of urate of ammonia instead of urea. In urea CN_2H_4O, the ratio of nitrogen to carbon is as 2 to 1; whereas in urate of ammonia $C_5N_5H_7O_3$, it is as 1 to 1, so that for an equal elimination of nitrogen, the quantity of carbon discharged from the kidneys of birds in the form of urate of ammonia, is twice as great as that discharged from the kidneys of mammals in the form of urea. Now, we have seen that the proportion of the carbon of nitrogenised tissue $C_8N_2H_xO_y$, excreted by the kidneys of carnivorous mammals is $\frac{1}{8}$ of the whole, and accordingly that excreted by the kidneys of carnivorous birds in the form of urate of ammonia will be $\frac{1}{4}$ of the whole. In other words, by the production of urate of ammonia instead of urea, the lungs of birds are required to discharge only $\frac{3}{4}$ instead of $\frac{7}{8}$ of the waste carbon resulting from the metamorphosis of nitrogenous tissue, although, as I have already observed, a larger amount of nitrogenous tissue has to be transformed in order to liberate the same amount of energy. On this view the comparatively large kidneys of birds and insects will have reference not only to the absolute amount of tissue metamorphosed, but also to the relative increase in the proportion of carbon excreted by their kidneys to that excreted by their lungs.

(153.) To sum up the foregoing considerations, we perceive that the amount of force lost by the metamorphosis of a given quantity of tissue, or indirectly of food, into the carbonic oxide constituent of uric acid, instead of into carb-anhydride, is less than might at first be supposed—that the amount of force gained by the conversion of a given quantity of oxygen into the carbonic oxide constituent of uric acid, instead of into carb-anhydride, is very large—and lastly, that by the production of the carbonic oxide constituent of uric acid, instead of carb-anhydride, the kidneys of birds are enabled to act vicariously for the lungs as excernents of a portion of that carbon which in mammals is habitually discharged by the lungs.

How far this production and excretion of urate of ammonia, instead of urea and carb-anhydride, may depend upon an inadequate pulmonic oxidation of the blood of birds, not entirely compensated for by its considerable systemic oxidation; and how far upon the connection with the portal circulation and inferior type of structure of their kidneys, as well as upon the small amount of water they drink and discharge, whereby their blood is less constantly and thoroughly washed than is the blood of mammals, are questions which it is for the physiologist rather than the chemist to determine.

(154). I can scarcely venture to conclude this course of lectures on 'Animal Chemistry' without saying a few words upon the influence exerted on tissue-metamorphosis by those chemical agents which are usually included in the class of alterative medicines. Although our acknowledged ignorance of the mode in which medicines produce their effects is made a standing reproach to medical art, only by those who, ignorant of their ignorance, wrongly conceive that in other scientific arts—that of the chemist, for example—the use of the different agents employed has really ceased to be empiric, and become dependent upon abstract principle, still it will not do for us to regard the therapeutic actions of different medicines as ultimate facts with which we must ever rest contented, but rather as difficult problems inviting a more competent investigation, and destined some day or other to yield to our inquiries. The subject, however, is too remote from even the present widely-extended boundary of scientific knowledge—the path from the known to the unknown is yet too lengthy and intricate—to warrant us in expecting any immediate, or, indeed, proximate resolution of the darkness by which it is surrounded. In the belief, however, that even a little gleam of light, insignificant in relation to more advanced researches, may not prove altogether worthless here, I beg respectfully to suggest the following points for your consideration. It will be found, I think, that those mineral substances which act more especially as alteratives, actually are, and necessarily ought to be, characterised, not by their chemical energy, but by their chemical mobility; and I do not know that I can make my meaning better evident than by directing your attention to the chemical properties of iodine in comparison with those of its intimate congener, chlorine. As I shall presently show you, both elements possess in a striking degree the property of oxidising various substances which resist the action of ordinary oxygen; and this observation leads me to make a few preliminary remarks upon the process of oxidation in general.

(155.) It is well known that many oxidisable bodies which are unable or scarcely able to combine directly with free oxygen, can nevertheless combine on the instant with oxygen that is already in a state of combination. It seems, indeed, as if the fact of previous combination conferred upon the transferable oxygen a greater activity or tendency to unite with other bodies. Of this peculiarity of behaviour, the non-oxidation or slow oxidation of sulphurous acid H_2SO_3, into sulphuric acid H_2SO_4, by mere exposure to oxygen or air, and its rapid oxidation by means of certain hyper-oxygenised compounds, such as the peroxides of hydrogen and nitrogen, affords us an excellent illustration. I have here a freshly made solution of sulphurous acid, and to it I add a little chloride of barium, which, you observe, does not in the least disturb its transparency, thereby showing its freedom from any trace of sulphuric acid. I now draw a rapid current of air through the mixed liquid, but with no obvious effect. The sulphurous acid and oxygen, despite their agitation together, remain sulphurous acid and oxygen, instead of combining with one another to form sulphuric acid. Accordingly, we have not enough sulphuric acid produced to afford even a turbidity with the previously added barium-salt, although, by a prolonged agitation with one another, some sulphuric acid would be slowly formed. I now divide the mixed solution of sulphurous acid and chloride of barium, and to one portion add a little peroxide of hydrogen, when immediately we get a copious white precipitate of sulphate of barium, showing that the sulphurous acid, which would not unite with the free oxygen of the air, has united at once with the combined oxygen of the peroxide, thus :—

Sulphurous	Hydric perox.		Sulphuric		Water
H_2SO_3	$H_2O.O$	=	H_2SO_4	+	H_2O,

The second half of the liquid I now pour into this bottle, charged, as you see, with brown fumes of peroxide of nitrogen, and agitate the whole for an instant or so; when the rapid oxidation of the sulphurous acid is rendered evident, in this as in the former experiment, by an abundant precipitation of sulphate of barium, while the brown peroxide is simultaneously reduced to the state of colourless oxide of nitrogen, thus:—

Sulphurous		Nitric perox.		Sulphuric		Nitric oxide
H_2SO_3	+	$NO.O$	=	H_2SO_4	+	NO.

(156.) The peroxides of hydrogen and nitrogen, therefore, are deoxidised by sulphurous acid in a precisely similar manner; but we shall find a great difference of behaviour in the protoxides resulting from their respective deoxidations. Thus the protoxide of hydrogen, or water, is a far more difficult substance to peroxidise than sulphurous acid itself. It is only, indeed, by a series of indirect processes that we are able to fasten on to its molecule an additional atom of oxygen, so as to convert it into the peroxide; and this added atom of oxygen is retained with such a feeble force, that it is frequently thrown off in the gaseous state, and constantly given up with the greatest readiness to any oxidisable substance, such as sulphurous acid. Although, therefore, it seems strange that sulphurous acid should not readily absorb oxygen from the air, there is nothing strange in its taking away the additional loosely combined oxygen existing in peroxide of hydrogen. But the oxide of nitrogen resulting from the deoxidation of *its* peroxide is a very different kind of body. Of all compounds known to chemists it is the one which absorbs free oxygen with the greatest avidity. No sooner, for instance, do I open the stopper of this bottle than the contained nitric oxide which we reduced from the peroxide a few minutes ago, combines at once with fresh oxygen from the air to become reconverted into the brown peroxide; and, on now closing the bottle and agitating its contents, the sulphurous acid, which is of itself unable to combine directly with atmospheric oxygen, instantly robs the peroxide of nitrogen of the oxygen which it had absorbed directly from the atmosphere, as in the ordinary manufacture of sulphuric acid, thus :—

Sulphurous		Oxygen		Sulphurous		Oxygen
H_2SO_3	+	O	=	H_2SO_3	+	O.

Nitric oxide		Oxygen		Nitric peroxide		
NO	+	O	=	NO_2.		

Sulphurous		Nitric perox.		Sulphuric		Nitric oxide
H_2SO_3	+	NO_2	=	H_2SO_4	+	NO.

(157.) Nitric oxide and peroxide, then, are the types of chemically mobile compounds. Regarded as a reducing agent, there are many more powerful de-oxygenants than the oxide; regarded as an oxidising agent, there are many more energetic oxygenants than the peroxide; but there are no two associated bodies known to chemists which respectively absorb and evolve oxygen with so much facility. As remarked by Laurent, 'There is no substance which presents such singular properties as nitric oxide. . . . It is, perhaps, the only body which, in the dry state and at the ordinary temperature, can combine suddenly with oxygen. The combination, moreover, takes place without the evolution of heat, and the body which results, far from retaining the oxygen that it has so readily absorbed, is perhaps of all bodies the one which is deoxidised most easily.' Now, while chlorine may be compared to peroxide of hydrogen, it is the sort of chemical mobility manifested by the oxides of nitrogen, which is characteristic of iodine, and, I believe, of most mineral alteratives. Iodide of hydrogen or potassium is, like nitric oxide, a facile reducing agent, and free iodine or hypiodite of potassium, like peroxide of nitrogen, a facile oxygenant—so that wherever the iodine travels it is capable of influencing the processes of oxidation there going on—absorbing oxygen where there is excess, delivering active oxygen where there is deficiency—just as our nitric compound absorbs oxygen from the air and delivers it up to the sulphurous acid. It is this chemical mobility of iodine, then, which chiefly distinguishes it from its more active congeners, chlorine and bromine. The general chemical relationship of these three elements to one another is most striking. With the probable exception of fluorine, they possess the exclusive property of uniting with hydrogen in the proportion of volume to volume,—the combinations, moreover, being unattended by any condensation. Again, the resulting compounds—namely, the hydrochloric, hydrobromic, and hydriodic—acids are all gaseous, all fuming, all soluble in water, and all producible by similar reactions.

(158.) Another common property by which chlorine, bromine, and iodine are characterised, is their marked activity when in the free state, which very greatly exceeds that of oxygen under similar conditions. In my last lecture I showed you the violent action of chlorine on metallic copper, upon which ordinary oxygen is, as you know, almost without action; and I have only a few minutes back referred to the little effect exerted by free oxygen upon various oxidisable bodies. But chlorine, bromine, and iodine act upon different metals, pseudo-metals, and compounds, with the greatest readiness; and, indeed, several of the iodides contained in the London and British Pharmacopœias are directed to be made by treating the respective metals at once with iodine. Lastly, all three elements are capable of acting as oxidising agents in cases where free oxygen is altogether, or almost, impotent. They contain no oxygen, it is true, and are, on the contrary, so far as our present knowledge goes, simple or elementary bodies. Nevertheless, in the presence of water, they act as very powerful oxygenants by uniting with the hydrogen of the water, and so liberating its pre-combined, and consequently active oxygen. Thus, on adding chlorine, bromine, and iodine respectively to the clear mixture of sulphurous acid and chloride of barium contained in these three glasses, we have in each instance an immediate precipitate of sulphate of barium from the oxidation of the sulphurous acid—just as in our former experiments with the peroxides of hydrogen and nitrogen—the reaction being as follows:—

INDIRECT OXIDATION BY HALOGENS. 151

Sulphurous	Water	Chlorine		Sulphuric	Chlorhydric
H_2SO_3 +	H_2O +	Cl_2	=	H_2SO_4 +	$2HCl$.

Here, again, I have three white magmas of protoxide of lead, with an excess of dilute alkali, exposed freely to the air; and this protoxide, although it does not absorb oxygen from the air, yet when treated with chlorine, bromine, and iodine, is at once oxidised more or less completely into the brown peroxide, as you perceive, thus:—

Lead-oxide	Water	Bromine		Lead-perox.	Bromhydric
PbO +	H_2O +	Br_2	=	PbO_2 +	$2HBr$.

Lastly, I have in these three glasses some solution of blue indigo exposed to the air, but unoxidised by the air. On adding chlorine, bromine, and iodine, however, it is at once bleached or oxidised into isatin, thus:—

Indigo	Water	Iodine		Isatin	Iodhydric
C_8H_5NO +	H_2O +	I_2	=	$C_8H_5NO_2$ +	$2HI$.

(159.) In all these particulars, then, chlorine, bromine, and iodine, though so different in their medicinal action, resemble one another to the greatest extent chemically. Now let us see what are their chemical, and, I may add, physical differences. I will first advert to their combining proportions, or the relative weights of each of them, which unite with 1 part by weight of hydrogen. These are indicated by the numbers 35·5, 80, and 127, which also represent their respective specific gravities, when in the gaseous state. You will observe that the proportional number of bromine is intermediate between that of chlorine and iodine, and indeed approximates very closely to the true arithmetic mean, $\frac{242·5}{3} = 80·8$, thus:—

Cl	35·5	Chlorine.
Br	80	Bromine.
I	127	Iodine.
	242·5	

The circumstance of these numbers also expressing the chemical equivalents of the several elements leads to some curious medico-chemical considerations. Thus, bearing in mind that sodium and potassium are related to one another in much the same way as are chlorine and iodine, though not perhaps quite so intimately, it will follow that 58·5 parts of common salt or chloride of sodium and 74·5 parts of chloride of potassium are the chemical equivalents of 166 parts of iodide of potassium, thus:—

NaCl	=	23	+	35·5	=	58·5
KCl	=	39	+	35·5	=	74·5
KI	=	39	+	127	=	166·0

Chemically, then, 58·5 parts of chloride of sodium are just as efficient as 166 parts of iodide of potassium; but while most of us, I suppose, are in the habit of taking fifty or sixty grains of common salt twice or three times a day, none of us, I conceive, would like to take 166 grains of iodide of potassium even once in the same period.

(160.) The gradational difference subsisting between the atomic weights or volume-weights of chlorine, bromine, and iodine is typical of all their chemical and physical differences. Thus their usual states of aggregation, gaseous, liquid, and solid, and the colours of their respective gases or vapours, green, orange, and violet, are sequential to one another; while, in a chemical point of view, we notice a successive decrease of the force with which they respectively enter into and remain in combination with most other bodies. Thus chlorine combines directly with hydrogen upon simple exposure of the mixed gases to ordinary daylight, and the resulting chlorhydric acid is an extremely stable body. But the direct combination of bromine with hydrogen takes place very imperfectly, and then only at a red heat, while the bromine of the resulting compound is liberated with comparative ease. Further, the direct combination of iodine with hydrogen is almost impracticable, while the iodhydric acid resulting from the indirect combination of the two elements is readily decomposed even by the action of atmospheric oxygen, thus: $2HI + O = H_2O + I_2$. Now, it is this feebleness of the force with which iodine enters into certain combinations, and consequent facility with which it is separated from such combinations, that give it that peculiar mobility to which I have already adverted. The chief chemical difference, indeed, between chlorine and iodine seems to be that chlorine in the free state is far more active than iodine, and iodine in the combined state far more mobile than chlorine, while in both respects bromine occupies an intermediate position. Hence, on adding a little bromine-water to this solution of iodide of potassium, the bromine expels the iodine, $KI + Br = KBr + I$, which, dissolving in the chloroform I had previously introduced, manifests itself to you by the production of a beautiful violet-coloured stratum at the bottom of the tube. Similarly, when I add a little chlorine water to this solution of bromide of potassium, the chlorine expels the bromine, $KBr + Cl = KCl + Br$, which dissolving in the previously introduced ether, floats on the surface as an orange-brown layer; so that while bromine expels iodine, chlorine expels bromine, and *à fortiori* iodine, from their respective combinations. Accordingly, we may regard $35\cdot5$ parts of chlorine as an energetic representative of 127 parts of iodine; but it is this very energy of chlorine, I conceive, which disqualifies it for acting medicinally as an alterative. On account of its intense chemical affinity, it unites more rapidly and forcibly than iodine with the different basyloïds it may chance to encounter, but directly it has entered into combination with them, its work is done, its action ceases. The resulting chloride of sodium, or other chloride, is of so stable a nature as to be impressionable only to violent chemical agencies; whereas, iodine, on the other hand, forming very unstable compounds, is constantly, with every change of circumstance, entering into a fresh state of liberation or combination—constantly effecting fresh oxidising or deoxidising actions.

(161.) I have already given you several illustrations of the oxidising action of free iodine, and ought, perhaps, to mention one or two instances of the correlative deoxidising action of combined iodine. You will remember that succinic acid, which is so to speak, the oxalic acid of the butyric group, is intimately associated with certain other members of the same group, thus:—

Succinic Sub-group
$C_4H_4O_4$ Fumaric.
$C_4H_6O_4$ Succinic.
$C_4H_6O_5$ Malic.
$C_4H_6O_6$ Tartaric.

Now tartaric acid, when heated with aqueous iodide of hydrogen or iodhydric acid, is converted into malic acid with liberation of iodine, thus:—

Tartaric   Iodhydric   Malic   Iodine   Water
$C_4H_6O_6 \; + \; 2HI \; = \; C_4H_6O_5 \; + \; I_2 \; + \; H_2O.$

Similarly the malic and fumaric acids are reducible into succinic acid by means of iodhydric acid, thus:—

Malic   Iodhydric   Succinic   Iodine   Water
$C_4H_6O_5 \; + \; 2HI \; = \; C_4H_6O_4 \; + \; I_2 \; + \; H_2O.$

Fumaric   Iodhydric   Succinic   Iodine
$C_4H_4O_4 \; + \; 2HI \; = \; C_4H_6O_4 \; + \; I_2.$

Accordingly, we find that while free iodine, acting as an oxidising agent, produces iodhydric acid, this same acid, acting as a deoxidising agent, reproduces free iodine. Here, for instance, I have some iodhydric acid, mixed with a little starch to show the results of the experiment. I now add to the iodhydric acid some peroxidised substance, which it immediately reduces, with liberation of iodine, as shown by the blue colour of the liquid. I now add to the free iodine some suboxidised substance, which it immediately oxidises, with reconversion into iodhydric acid, as shown by the disappearance of the blue colour. On now adding some more of the peroxidised substance, I re-liberate the iodine, and, on afterwards adding some more of the suboxidised substance, I reproduce the iodhydric acid, and so on *ad infinitum.* The characteristic chemical property of iodine consists, therefore, in the comparative feebleness of its affinities, or in the loose state of combination with which it is capable of being retained by other bodies; so that, while the more energetic chlorine acts once for all, the less energetic iodine .is acting and reacting upon every occasion. Accordingly, while it makes all the difference whether we employ free chlorine or chloride of sodium to produce the therapeutic effects of chlorine, it makes very little difference whether we employ free iodine or iodide of potassium to produce the therapeutic effects of iodine. Wherever the element travels, it either oxidises or deoxidises, accordingly as it comes into contact with bodies more or less oxidisable than itself, at that particular moment. It acts, in fact, not only as a converter of inactive or free, into active or combined oxygen, but also as a conveyer of oxygen from wherever it is in excess to wherever it is in deficiency.

(162.) Now, what is true of iodine and its compounds is also true of the compounds of mercury, of arsenic, and of another metal whose alterative action is manifested in almost an opposite fashion,—namely, iron. Considered chemically, the compounds of these three metals are, perhaps, the most constantly impressionable of any with which we are acquainted. In the laboratory, and even in the factory, we habitually avail ourselves of mercuric, arsenic, and ferric compounds as oxygenants, and of mercurous, arsenious, and ferrous compounds as deoxygenants or reducants. The relationship between chlorine and iodine is parallel to that between phosphorus and arsenic,—the phosphoric and arsenic acids, for instance, though so different in their therapeutic effects, being the strict chemical analogues of one another. Phosphorus is a far more active element than arsenic, and its combinations are far more stable. Phosphate of sodium, once formed, is like common salt; a stable innocuous body; while arseniate of sodium, like iodide of potassium, is an active body, because of its instability—because of the liability of its arsenical constituent to affect and be affected by the chemical actions taking place everywhere throughout the body. I am far, of course, from thinking that this susceptibility to oxidation and deoxidation furnishes a complete solution of the medicinal efficacy of alterative salts. But when we remember that every change produced in the composition of any part of the animal body is a chemical change, necessitating a correlative change in the composition of the reacting substance, it is obvious that we must look for alterative agents among that class of substances which are most susceptible of chemical change; and I would add further, that an explanation of the different kinds of alterative effect producible by different classes of compounds, as of mercury and iron, for instance, is, doubtless, to be sought for in the different chemical habitudes of the respective elements.

(163.) A few words upon the effect of alkalies in promoting oxidation. I mentioned in my last lecture the peculiar decomposition of animal substances resulting from their treatment with caustic alkali, and consisting in an oxidation of their carbonous at the expense of their hydrogenous constituents. Now, this action is apparently determined by the tendency which exists among differently characterised elements to arrange themselves in stable groupings, and more particularly to form stable oxi-salts. The presence of alkali rendering the formation of such salts possible, by furnishing the necessary base, we find that under treatment with caustic potash KHO, for instance, the carbon of organic matter is oxidised into various acids, which appear in the form of their respective potassium-salts; while the excessive hydrogen of the organic matter, together with that of the potash employed, is liberated in the gaseous state, as already exemplified by the reaction of caustic potash with oil of bitter almonds. As a result of this tendency, then, we obtain, as I have previously remarked, very similar products by fusing animal substances with caustic alkalies, and by submitting them to the action of powerful oxygenants. It is observable, however, as well in artificial as in natural processes, that the ultimate effects of a gentle chemical action are often more complete than the immediate results of a comparatively violent one; and it is to this more gentle action of alkalies that I would now direct your attention. We find that many organic substances, which of themselves are scarcely affected by exposure to oxygen or air, undergo a complete and even somewhat rapid oxidation under the influence of alkalies, the tendency of their constituent carbon to become oxidised, otherwise inferior to that of their constituent hydrogen, becoming intensified, apparently because of the opportunity afforded by the presence of the alkali for the formation of salts instead of acids.

(164.) Be the explanation, however, what it may, the fact is unquestionable, and readily admits of experimental illustration. For instance, I have in this porcelain dish the watery solution of a substance well known to photographers as pyrogallic acid, though its acidity is of such a feeble character that it is nowadays more frequently spoken of by chemists under the neutral appellation of pyrogallin. At present, the solution in the dish, though exposed freely to the air for upwards of an hour, has not undergone any appreciable oxidation. I now moisten the interior of this long tube with a little aqueous potash, and invert it in the solution, when the commencing oxidation of the dissolved pyrogallin is manifested to you by its almost immediate assumption of a brown-black colour, followed by the gradual rising up of the black liquid in the tube, through an absorption of the oxygen of the contained air. The pyrogallin, which did not become oxidised in any appreciable degree so long as there was no alkali present, now becomes oxidised with considerable rapidity, as you observe, yielding among other products acetate, oxalate and carbonate of potassium. Other familiar illustrations of this action of alkalies are afforded us in the employment of lime to promote the destructive oxidation of dead bodies, and as a manure to destroy the organic matter of peaty soils. Some very interesting results have also been obtained by Gorup-Besanez, who found that glycerin, sugar, leucine, hippuric acid, oxalic acid, and the fatty and aromatic acids, which of themselves were unacted upon by ozonised air, underwent a very complete oxidation when submitted to the same reagent in the presence of caustic or even carbonated alkali. Benzoic acid, for instance, which results from the violent oxidation of animal matter, and consistently resists the action of very powerful oxygenants, undergoes a complete and somewhat speedy oxidation when submitted in alkaline solution to the action of ozone. And in some of these oxidations the curious circumstance was noted, that between the original substance—stearic acid $C_{18}H_{36}O_2$, or benzoic acid $C_7H_6O_2$, for instance—and the final carbonic acid, no intermediate products could be detected. It seemed, indeed, as if portion after portion of the original substance was completely oxidised and broken up into separate molecules of carbonic acid, instead of the entire substance undergoing a gradual oxidation and simplification, by the successive burning off of its constituent carbon-atoms, one after another, into carbonic acid. With such facts as these before us, I would submit that the so-called resolvent action of alkalies upon the animal economy, like that of iodine, is a direct consequence of the peculiar chemical characterisation by which they are enabled to act as oxidising agents.

(165.) Despite, however, the interest of these questions, upon which I have been able to bestow but a very hasty notice, I must now break off their discussion altogether, and regretfully take my leave of you. In bringing this course of lectures to a conclusion, I have to thank you, my indulgent auditors, and more particularly the President and Fellows of the College, for the kind encouragement which your continued presence has afforded me. I am aware how far short my lectures have fallen of that degree of excellence which I had hoped to attain, and you had a right to expect; and how much the measure of success which has attended them must be attributed to the intrinsic merit of the subject, and your good-natured willingness to be pleased with its expounder. I have endeavoured throughout to bring prominently before you the dynamical idea of organic chemistry, as connected with changes of composition. I have shown you that, in the organism of the plant, carbonic acid and water are submitted to a constant deoxidising change, whereby they become successively converted into more and more complex bodies, many of which we are now able to produce, all of which we hope some day to produce, by similar processes in the laboratory; that the change in composition undergone by carbonic acid and water is attended by a storing-up of solar force in the resulting products, and that the correlative change in composition undergone by these products into water and carbonic acid is attended by a liberation of the force stored up in them; that in every organ of the animal body oxidation is continually taking place to furnish that organ with the force necessary for the performance both of its nutritive acts and external manifestations; that the juice of every gland and muscle is crowded with oxidised products of its own metamorphosis, similar to, or even identical with, those procurable by an artificial oxidation of the selfsame tissue out of the body; that inasmuch as the exercise of every function of the living body is attended by, and consequent upon, a change of chemical composition, the investigation of every action of the body, even of those which are the most mechanical, becomes to a large extent a chemical question; and lastly, that while perversions of nutrition, perversions of metamorphosis, and the modifying influence of remedies, are many-sided subjects which may be viewed from many different aspects, he must have but a very imperfect and one-sided view of these subjects, who leaves the chemical aspect altogether out of his consideration.

INDEX.

ACE

ACETAMIDE, residues of, 27
Acetic acid, congeners of, 47
— — inflammability of, 34
— — synthesis of, 59-91
Acetonitrile, residues of, 27
Acetylene, characters of, 90
— hydrogenation of, 88
— synthesis of, 88
Acids and amides, mutual metamorphoses of, 118
Acids, oxidation by, 117
Alcohol, synthesis of, 89
Alcohols, synthetic plasticity of, 82
Aldehydes, acidifiability of, 111
— examples of, 111
— properties of, 110
Alkalies, oxidation by, 157
Allantoine, a diureide, 136
Allophan, a polymerone, 43
Allophanic acid, a mon-ureide, 133
Alloxan, a mon-ureide, 136
Alterative action of iodine, 155
Alteratives, action of alkaline, 156
— action of metallic, 155
Amides, cyanuric, 19
— mineral, 16
— organic, 17
Amid-hypoxanthine, or guanine, 139
Ammonia, a pabulum for plants, 52
— acetate, dehydration of, 27
— nitrogen a proxy for, 55
— oxalate, dehydration of, 29
— type, 10
Aniline, synthesis of, 94
Animal products, list of, 5
Animality, characteristics of, 77
An-ureide acids, 131
Aplones, combination of, 55

CHE

Aplone molecules, 30
Aromatic acids of flesh, 115
— — series of, 34
Asparagine, decomposition of, 92
Atomic heats, 14
Atomic weights, table of, 15

BARBITURIC ACID, a mon-ureide, 144
Benzamide, origin of, 37
Benzoglycolic acid, origin of, 38
Benzoic acid, synthesis of, 94
— group, 35
Bile-acids, polymerones, 44
Birds, tissue-oxidation in, 144
Butyric acid group, 32
— — synthesis of, 92

CARB-ANHYDRIDE, carbon from, 63
— reduction of, 62
Carbon-atoms, conjunction of, 51
— — separation of, 49
Carbon, combination-heat of, 100
— combustion of, 61
Carbon-compounds, complexity of, 23
— — number of, 23
Carbonic acid, metamorphoses of, 84
— — series, 36
Carbonic oxide, combination-heat of, 142
— — synthesis by, 83
Chemical action, nature of, 4
— — of medicines, 146
Chemical actions of plant-life, 63
— elements, 7

CHE

Chemical powers, limit to? 58
— types, 7
Chemistry, dynamical, 4
— first principles of, 2
— organic, analytic, 49
— — synthetic, 60
— statical, 3
— synthetic, economy of, 96
— — results of, 95
Chlorides, metallic, 14
— typical, 13
Chlorine, activity of, 152
Classification of uric acid products, 131
Coal-tar colours, synthesis of, 95
Combination of hydrogen and carbon, direct, 89
Combination-heat of carbon, 100
— — carbonic oxide, 142
— — hydrogen, 100
— — zinc, 72
Combustion, solar heat restored by, 75
Corrosive sublimate, formula of, 14
Cross-bow, force of, 70
Cyanogen, production of, 28
— residues of, 29
Cyanuric amides, 19

DEHYDROGENATION of uric acid, 129
Diamerone, myricin, a, 42
— spermaceti, a, 41
— urea, a, 41
Diamerones, examples of, 40
— the fats, 42
— monureide, 135
Diamide, urea, a, 18
Diureide, allantoine, a, 136
— mycomelic acid, a, 136
Dynamical chemistry, 4
Dynamics of uric acid, 142

EDUCTS and products, 22
Electrolysis, heat absorbed in, 74
— nature of, 71
— of water, 73
Elements, chemical, 7
Empiric formula of tyrosine, 120
Energy, actual, 7
— potential, 71

HEA

Ethylene, synthesis of, 88
Excretion of urates by birds, 141
— — by reptiles, 141

FATS, the, diamerones, 42
— oxidation-products of, 48
Fatty acid series, 31
— acids of flesh, 114
— — properties of, 33
— — series of diatomic, 36
— alcohol series, 35
— aldehyde series, 35
Flesh, aromatic acids of, 115
Flesh-oxidation, acids of, 113
Foot-pound, meaning of, 104
Force absorbed in nutrition, 76
— indestructibility of, 76
— solar origin of muscular, 107
Formation of peroxides, 148
Formic acid, history of, 85
— compounds, 85

GALLIC ACID, synthesis of, 94
Gelatin, sugar of, 119
Glycerin, synthesis of, 92
Glycocine, occurrence of, 119
— of hippuric acid, 38
— synthesis of, 91
Grape-sugar, synthesis of? 93
Group benzoic, 35
— butyric, 32
— propionic, 31
Group-terms, principal, 32
Guanidine, an amide, 19
— production of, 139
Guanine, or amid-hypoxanthine, 139

HALOGENS, differences between, 151
— mutual resemblances of, 150
— oxidation by, 151
Heat absorbed in electrolysis, 74
— — in vegetation, 75
— — and motion, correlation of, 68
— intensity of, 101
— of friction, 69
— quantity of, 101
— solar, restored by combustion, 75
— transformations of, 68

HEA

Heat, unit of, 100
Heats, atomic, 14
Hippuric acid, constitution of, 36
— — decompositions of, 37
— — glycocine of, 38
— — residues of, 39
Homologous series, 33
Hydrates, mineral, 16
— organic, 17
Hydrides, typical, 13
Hydrocarbons, series of aromatic, 35
Hydrochloric acid type, 7
Hydrogen and carbon, direct combination of, 89
Hydrogen, combination-heat of, 100
— combustion of, 61
Hydrogenation of acetylene, 88
Hypoxanthine, occurrence of, 137

IGNITION of platinum wire, 73
Indestructibility of force, 76
Indigo, in urine, 122
— nature of, 121
Intensity of heat, 101
Iodhydric acid, reductions by, 153
Iodine, alterative action of, 154
— mobility of, 149

KILOGRAM-METRE, meaning of, 104
Kreatine, a polymerone, 44

LACTIC ACID, synthesis of, 92
Leucine, association of, with tyrosine, 116
— distribution of, 116
— formation of, 5, 117
List of animal products, 5

MALIC ACID, synthesis of, 93
Mannite, production of, 51
Manures, nitrites as, 54
Marsh-gas, derivatives of, 88
— — production of, 87
Matter, kinds of, 3
Medicines, chemical action of, 146
Mesoxalic acid, deoxidation of, 133
— — oxidation of, 131

ORG

Metallic alteratives, action of, 155
— chlorides, 14
Metamorphoses of carbonic acid, 84
Methylamine, 40
Methyl-compounds, 86
Methyluramine, a polymerone, 45
Mineral amides, 16
— hydrates, 16
Mobility of iodine, 149
— of nitric oxides, 149
Molecular volumes, 11
Molecules, aplone, 30
— nitrogen, 52
— polymerone, 30
Mon-ureide, allophanic acid, a, 133
— — alloxan, a, 136
— — barbituric acid, a, 136
Monureides, dehydration of, 133
Motion, arrest of, 68
— and heat, correlation of, 68
— transmission of, 69
— unit of, 103
Muscle-heat and motion, correlation of, 106
— oxidation, economy of, 105
— — results of, 98
Muscular activity, conditions of, 97
— force, solar origin of, 107
Mutual metamorphoses of acids and amides, 118
Mycomelic acid, a diureide, 136
Myricin, a diamerone, 42

NITRIC OXIDES, mobility of, 149
Nitriles, acidifiability of, 113
— nature of, 112
Nitrites as manures, 54
Nitrogen a proxy for ammonia, 55
— molecules, 52
— production of, 54
Nitrous acid, formation of, 53
— — reduction of, 53
Nutrition, force absorbed in, 76

ORGANIC AMIDES, 17
— chemistry, analytic, 49
— — synthetic, 60
— groups and series, 30
— hydrates, 17

ORG

Organic proximate principles, 22
Oxalate of ammonia, dehydration of, 29
Oxalic acid, oxidation of, 132
— — series, 36
— — synthesis of, 92
Oxalurate of calcium, in urine, 135
Oxidation by acids, 117
— by alkalies, 157
— by fused potash, 117
— by peroxides, 147
— slow or rapid, 102
Oxygen, evolution of, by plants, 50

PEROXIDES, formation of, 148
— oxidation by, 147
— reduction of, 147
Phenol in urine, 123
Plant life, chemical actions of, 63
Plants, ammonia, a pabulum for, 52
— evolution of oxygen by, 50
Platinum wire, ignition of, 73
Polymerone molecules, 30
— allophan, a, 43
— kreatine, a, 44
— methylamine, a, 45
— taurine, a, 43
— uric acid, a, 128
Polymerones, the bile acids, 44
— examples of, 43
Populin, composition of, 25
— residues of, 27
Potash, oxidation by fused, 117
Processes, animal and vegetable, 64
Products and educts, 22
— formation of vegetable, 79
Propionic group, 31
Proximate principles, organic, 22
Prussic acid, production of, 86
— — vital origin of? 58
Pseudo-uric acid, production of, 140

QUANTITY of heat, 101

RATIO of urea to carbonic acid, 99
Reduction of peroxides, 147
Residues, doctrine of, 26

SYN

SALICIC ACID, synthesis of, 94
— compounds, 121
Salicin, composition of, 25
— hydration of, 26
— residues of, 26
Saligenin, reaction of, 25
Salisuric acid in urine, 123
Sarcosine, synthesis of, 91
Series of aromatic acids, 34
— — hydrocarbons, 35
— carbonic acid, 36
— of fatty acids, 31
— — — diatomic, 36
— — alcohols, 35
— — aldehydes, 35
— — oxalic acid, 36
Spermaceti, a diamerone, 41
Statical chemistry, 3
Steam-engine, principle of, 68
Sub-oxidised tissue-products, 108
Succinic acid, synthesis of, 92
Sugar of gelatin, 21
Sugar, vital origin of? 57
Syntheses, continuous, 81
Synthesis by carbonic oxide, 83
— of acetic acid, 59, 91
— — acetylene, 88
— — alcohol, 89
— — aniline, 94
— — benzoic acid, 94
— — butyric acid, 92
— — coal-tar colours, 95
— — ethylene, 88
— — gallic acid, 94
— — glycerin, 92
— — glycocine, 91
— — grape sugar? 93
— — lactic acid, 92
— — malic acid, 92
— — oxalic acid, 92
— — salicic acid, 94
— — sarcosine, 91
— — succinic acid, 92
— — tartaric acid, 92
— — taurine, 90
— — valeric acid, 93
Synthetic chemistry, economics of, 96
— — results of, 95
Synthetic methods, general, 81
— plasticity of alcohols, 82

INDEX.

TAB

TABLE of atomic weights, 15
— of uric acid products, 134
Tartaric acid, synthesis of, 92
Taurine, a polymerone, 43
— occurrence of, 6
— synthesis of, 90
Tissue-oxidation, in birds, 142
— — order of, 109
Tissue-products, sub-oxidised, 108
Trimethylamine, occurrence of, 87
Types, ammonia, 10
— chemical, 7
— hydrochloric acid, 7
— water, 9
Typical chlorides, 13
— hydrides, 12
Tyrosine, constitution of, 124
— distribution of, 116
— empiric formula of, 120
— formation of, 117

UNIT of heat, 100
— of motion, 103
Urea, a diamerone, 41
— a diamide, 18
— artificial production of, 86
— existence of, in uric acid? 129
Uric acid, a polymerone, 128
— — decomposition of, 129
— — dehydrogenation of, 129
— — dynamics of, 142
— — excretion, by birds, 141
— — — by reptiles, 141
— — existence of urea in? 129

ZIN

Uric acid, history of, 127
— — products, classification of, 131
— — — table of, 134
— — ultimate constitution of, 141
Urine, indigo in, 122
— oxalurate of calcium in, 135
— phenol in, 123
— salisuric acid in, 123
Uroxanic acid, production of, 140

VALERIC ACID, synthesis of, 93
Vegetation, experiments on, 50
— heat absorbed in, 75
Vital force, actions of? 56
— — hypothesis of, 77
— — sugar formed by? 57
— — views concerning, 57
Volumes, molecular, 11

WATER, electrolysis of, 73
— reduction of, 62
— type, 9
Wood-spirit, production of, 87

XANTHINE, history of, 138
— relations of, 138

ZINC, combination-heat of, 72
— combustion of, 71
— solution of, 72

LONDON
PRINTED BY SPOTTISWOODE AND CO.
NEW-STREET SQUARE

www.ingramcontent.com/pod-product-compliance
Lightning Source LLC
Chambersburg PA
CBHW020306170426

43202CB00008B/516